SUPER STRUCTURE

The Key to Unleashing the Power of Story

JAMES SCOTT BELL

Compendium Press

Compendium Press
Woodland Hills, CA

Contents

PART I

Structure Love

In *Write Your Novel From the Middle,* I provided a brief outline of Super Structure. This book fleshes out each of those steps, and provides tips and techniques for incorporating them into your own writing.

I've found it necessary to write this book because of an odd meme that's popped up in recent years. It holds that structure is a vile inhibitor of creativity, that story always suffers under its tyranny—as if story was Spartacus and structure the slave master who whips him around all day. Poor Spartacus! He can't possibly write his novel under these conditions!

It's a misguided notion that, if swallowed whole, will virtually guarantee a writer a future of miserable returns on his efforts.

Of course, not all writers care about generating income. There's a guy at my local Starbucks who writes poems on a manual typewriter. He writes the pages and hands them out and hopes for enough tips to buy some coffee.

He seems happy enough. He never thinks about structure.

Then there is the writer who came to me once with a project

that was a stinking mess. He protested that it was a labor of love and that there was some beautiful writing in it.

I agreed with him.

Then I told him no one is going to give a rip.

Because readers who pay money for fiction want to be hooked by a story. They want to get lost in it and care about the characters. They want to experience the tale emotionally, ride it out to the very end.

Which doesn't happen without structure.

As Exhibit A, I give you Dow Mossman.

Never heard of him? If you can find a DVD of the documentary *The Stone Reader*, hunt it down and watch it. It's about a writer of amazing natural gifts who could weave magic with his prose.

What he did not have was a handle on plot and structure, and therein lies the tragedy.

Dow Mossman wrote a novel called *The Stones of Summer*. It was published in 1972. It came out in hardcover with high hopes. It even got a favorable review in the *New York Times*.

But it tanked and quickly went out of print, destined to be forgotten.

Which is where the documentary comes in. I'll leave it to you to find out what happened. What interested me was this book. In conjunction with the movie, Barnes & Noble republished *The Stones of Summer* in a new, affordable hardcover edition. I bought it. I wanted to see if I'd missed a classic.

I will tell you this: Every page of that book is like some wild, Beat prose poem. There are word choices and metaphors and flights of literary fancy that delighted me.

For about two pages at a time.

Then my brain started to shut down. The wording was just too thick to sustain without something kind of crucial:

Structure.

And a skillfully woven plot.

The creativity and writing alone are simply not enough to sustain a satisfying reading experience.

Which is why the new edition of the book also tanked.

I say this with sympathy for the writer, who was obviously gifted with a genius for pure writing. He should have been a poet. Or come under the wing of an equally skilled editor who could have done for him what Max Perkins did for Thomas Wolfe.

What that editor would have taught Mr. Mossman is that the wonderful, amazing, vivid pictures and emotions in his mind needed to be given a *form* that would allow readers to share those things with him.

Translation Software

I call structure "translation software for your imagination." Structure takes the story you have in your heart and mind and transforms it into a narrative that readers can fall in love with.

Structure is story's best friend. Structure holds story's hand and fights off the dangers of confusion, frustration, and consternation in readers.

Story without structure is like skin without skeleton. Oil without a crankcase and combustion engine. Abbott without Costello.

If you disregard structure, you are like a Portuguese tourist trying to order Russian food at a Taiwainese restaurant.

Structure *unleashes* the power of story.

On my group blog, Kill Zone, commenter Tom Combs revealed his own epiphany about this. It is worth sharing in full (used by permission):

An aha! moment - my first fiction writing class seven years ago. Assignment - write a scene to be workshopped with classmates

I wrote a scene that was essentially autobiographical.

An ER doc/ helicopter flight physician flew to an attempted resuscitation scene where a young woman (daughter/mother) had been found on the bottom of a pool. She could not be saved.

The patient's body was flown back to the hospital and the family contacted and told only to "go to the ER." The scene I wrote described the ER doctor going to the family room to notify loved ones of the death.

The "scene" I wrote involved the dead woman's mother, her 10-year-old son and their displays of incredible grief and courage (esp the 10 y.o).

I could not have read the scene I wrote aloud without breaking down.

The feedback from one of the 3 students who provided feedback was, "I didn't like that the ER doctor was so cold."

I was speechless.

That lesson has stayed with me ... what is in the author's heart/mind is meaningless if it is not communicated by the words on the page. The challenge is to make/allow the reader to experience the meaning and emotion by reading printed words. That is the magic trick.

I've been working hard at that ever since. I much appreciate your instruction in use of the tools that help create the magic.

Creating magic takes work, not just play. To connect with readers is a matter of both sides of your brain working in concert. Don't use just half your brain. Leave that to the politicians.

You want to move readers, weave a dream, and leave people glad they found your books.

Super Structure is going to help you do that.

Clearing Up a Few Misconceptions

Let me set aside some of the bad raps tossed at good old structure.

First of all, structure is not "formulaic" in the way critics use that term. They mean structure "follows the numbers" but has no real heart.

That's a false definition.

Consider: what makes something a formula:

It *works*.

It's been tested and proven to be reliable.

If you go to a doctor and need a shot, you want him to give you what has been used over and over with success.

You don't want a doctor who says, "So, I was playing around this morning with some baking soda, water, pepper and chicken entrails, and I'd like to see if that'll work for you. What do you say?"

"Um, excuse me?"

"Sure! I was being creative! Just going for it! I wasn't tied down to old-fashioned ideas and formulas. They tried to put that in my head in med school. Well, I'm a rebel. And I'm much happier now! Roll up your sleeve, please."

Right. You want the formula.

Dear Mr. Bell: I attended your Plot and Structure seminar in Sherman Oaks a few years ago. I was writing my first romance novel at that time. 3 more books down the road, I was nominated for the 2014 Golden Heart and signed a 2 book deal with Montlake Romance. These successes are largely due to following your plot and structure formula. You were right - formulas really do work. Thanks! - Shelly Chester Alexander

ANOTHER FALSE ARGUMENT is that structure always leads to cardboard characters and clichéd plots.

Wrong.

In fact, when you use it right, structure creates plots that please and surprise, and are filled with unforgettable characters.

"But structure stifles play!" shout the skeptics.

No way. You start with your imagination and heart. You get fired up about telling a story because you have a plot idea (a "what if?") or a character idea, or both, and you're jazzed about seeing what happens.

Here is where you play. This is where you stoke the spark of an idea into a wildfire of original material.

At some point, however, you must bring form to this pile of raw brilliance or it will remain just that, a pile.

STILL ANOTHER CANARD about structure is that it takes the joy out of writing.

More hooey. In fact, when you know what structure is and does, it will excite you just as much as dancing through the playground of your wild side. You will know exactly what you're doing. There is nothing quite like the confidence of a craftsman who is practicing his trade with knowledge, experience, and love of what he does.

Finally, let me clear up this idea that utilizing structure is just a linear, mathematical process. This argument states that teachers of structure are trying to sell you on the idea that you can begin at square one and just follow along, step-by-step, all the way to the end, and have yourself a fully realized novel or screenplay.

More bunk.

Structure is flexible. You can utilize it at any time in the writing process. If you are an outlining type, you can indeed layout the skeleton of a solid plot from the get go.

If, on the other hand, you are a "seat of the pants" writer (or "pantser" for short), you can come to structure later in the process. Or you can use it when you get stuck in the thicket of the middle and need to find a way out.

One can even write an entire draft without any thought of structure, then upon reflection treat that draft as notes and deep material for a finished novel, which will happen when you finally put that material into a form readers can respond to.

The Concept of Signposts

I like to think of Super Structure as signpost scenes or beats. This is derived from the metaphor for writing a novel from E. L. Doctorow. He said it's like driving in the dark with the headlights on. You can see only as far along the highway as the lights allow, but once you drive further you see a little more.

To this I add that if you know what the next signpost is, you won't get lost or drive off a cliff.

So as you write, if you begin to wonder where to go next, Super Structure gives you the signpost up ahead. You drive toward that scene and you're right back on track.

For example, let's say you're 10,000 words into your novel and you've finished a chapter and you don't know what to write next. You feel lost. What do you do?

You look at Super Structure and determine that this is where the "Trouble Brewing" scene needs to be. You brainstorm that scene.

Maybe during the brainstorming you determine there's another scene that needs to come before it. Good! You have just given yourself even more direction along a good chunk of fiction highway.

You are writing a solid, creative, well-plotted book, signpost by signpost.

Turns out you're not lost at all!

In Defense of the Three Act Structure

In my early writing days I attended seminars by two of the noted story "gurus" of the day.

The gurus both began with remarks heaping scorn on the main idea of the guru who had preceded them both. This original guru was a strong proponent of the three-act structure, so much so that he called it the "paradigm" of all great movies.

One of the gurus shouted, "There is no ***** paradigm!"

Then, over the course of the next six hours, this guru expostulated his own view of story, which if you laid it out in linear fashion, broke down into *exactly three acts.*

The other guru did pretty much the same thing. His story model had a lot of moving parts, but when you stepped back for a look, those parts were arranged in a flow of three acts.

In point of fact, we are wired to receive things in three acts. Nature has set it up that way.

We are born and have a childhood (Act I). We spend most of our time in adulthood (Act II). If we live a long, full life, we enter the sunset of our years in Act III.

We begin our day in the morning. We get up, get our coffee (if we don't, we've really screwed up Act I), get ready for the rest of the day. If we're in-full time employment, we spend most of our day at work (Act II). We might go out for happy hour, which is the doorway to Act III, where we wind down and go to bed.

See the pattern?

At work we are given a problem to solve (Act I). We spend our time analyzing and figuring out what to do (Act II). We implement our solution (Act III).

Wells Root, a Hollywood screenwriter of the golden age and one of the first great screenwriting instructors, had an illustration in his book *Writing the Script* that pictured structure as a rushing river:

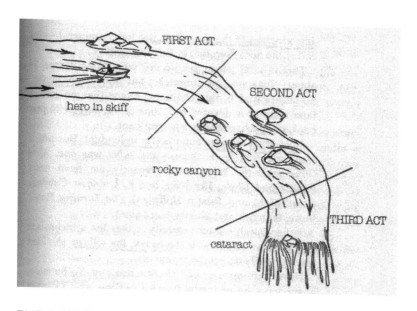

THE LEAD'S story has to begin somewhere, and it's best when he's in *motion* as shown here. The river of the story has a flow he's already caught up in.

Act II is where all the rocks and rapids are. Everything is picking up speed until, in Act III, events take us over a waterfall. We cannot stop and go backward. The end is nigh.

There is a certain inescapability about three acts.

That is, if you want to communicate.

So embrace it and let it unleash the power of story for your readers.

After all, they're wired for it.

"But I want to Experiment!"

No one's stopping you. You want to write an "experimental" novel? Go right ahead.

You will get a few readers for it, too.

Key word, *few*.

That's not a knock on experimental or literary forms that "break the rules." I'm all for artists doing what they want to do.

Just do it with eyes open. There's a reason there is no shelf at Barnes & Noble marked *Experimental*.

You can certainly self-publish and try things. Go for it.

But know this: even your experiments can be strengthened with an understanding of structure and having it in the back pocket of your writer's coveralls, ready to come out when needed.

So play all you like. Experiment. Have fun.

But review this book every now and then, too. I think you'll be glad you did.

2

On Plotting and Pantsing

In a very insightful look into the mind of pantser (at the great blog WriterUnboxed) author John Vorhaus admits to the terrors of the practice:

> So here's the consequence of that. I write these incredibly fast, very ragged, awfully ugly first drafts. I put a lot of ideas into play that I know will probably not pan out. I let loose ends live. I basically write anything I can think of, whether I can neatly tie it into the story or not. Unraveling the story problems, according to this model, can always come later.
>
> Trouble is: Later always comes.

And when it comes, there is massive work to do, especially with how to finish the thing:

> So there I am, stuck with a fast, ragged, ugly first draft, with loose ends sticking out all over, no clear sense of what I'm driving at thematically and – you can be sure of this – an ending that 100 percent does not work. My endings never work on the first draft because I simply don't have enough information yet to write them well. So I write them very badly,

then review what I've written and inevitably say this: "Okay, well, now I know what not to write."

Then I go to work.

The work turns into months and months of tearing apart and putting back together. The author is convinced that this is the only way to create his novel. Yet there is part of him that thinks there might be a better way:

Plus, no matter how easy or hard the work is, there's always something to learn about my process – something I can take away and apply next time. This time, for example, I learned that next time I really should try outlining.

I won't do it, of course, but it's nice to think I could.

In the comments, I suggest that he can.

You've described the pantsing vibe quite well, John. What you go through is what most of your kind do, with an emphasis on the length of time it takes to find the story you want to tell and the ending you want to reach.

Which means you are really an outliner after all. You're simply wedded to one, perhaps less efficient, method...

What I mean is, that "ragged, awfully ugly" stuff you call a "first draft" is really just a very large record of what your writer's mind has come up with .... which you then try to bring order to .... which amounts to outlining. You've just spent your months loving the initial creative process and the writing itself, which is understandable. But then the night sweats come. What if I've just spent months and months and there really isn't a book worthy story there after all?

The outliners, OTOH, are doing the same "ragged and ugly" thing, only in less time, so they can spend the bulk of their writing on a coherent first draft that can be edited for form and style. They pour out the raw material in their preliminary, creative mode (at least under the process I've come to use), before the actual writing of a draft. This is as much fun for us as the daily writing is for the pantser. This is where we let characters "grow" and "breathe" (I use a Voice Journal for this part, which is great fun.)

At the end we at least have the relief of knowing what our story is in days or weeks, not months. We know the stakes are high enough and the plot sufficiently fecund to proceed with confidence. The daily writing is about the fun of discovering how a scene develops, how characters advance agendas (which we already know), how they use dialogue as a weapon, and so forth.

All of which is subject to change if the need arises. I've had characters refuse to leave a setting. I've changed villains halfway through a story. But the framework is still there, the stakes and concept established, so I'm simply moving parts around. It's the same thing a pantser will eventually be forced to do. It's just that this part, the work part, isn't as fun for them. The pantser's motto might be, "Never do today what can be put off until tomorrow ... or six months from now!"

I think, bottom line, pantsers are most comfortable following Ray Bradbury's axiom, "We must stay drunk on writing so reality does not destroy us." Getting lost in the daily words, not knowing where they will lead, is intoxicating. Bringing order to chaos is more like work.

Bradbury, of course, was one of the great pantsers, but note: his best work was in short stories and novellas.

Okay, I feel like I've slipped into a legal brief here, arguing for my preferred method. I'm not as lawyerly as that. Among my students I've actually warned rigid outliners to loosen up. And I've also issued caveats to "pure pantsers."

I just want writers to be happy and efficient and successful ... which may mean trying a new way of doing things and becoming happier still!

To which my agent, friend, colleague and writing guru Donald Maass added:

> I agree with Jim. The pantser's first draft is an outline, or perhaps it's more like free writing, ideas waiting to be organized.
>
> I also agree with Jim that there are other ways for pantsers to work that will work for pantsers. The "squeezing out the stupid" method you describe strikes me as valid, but a slow way.
>
> There are alternatives.

In this book, I want to offer you an alternative. I love ya, pantsing friend. Let's see what we can do together.

"But I Want Twists and Turns No One Sees Coming!"

I've heard some writers say something along the following lines: "I just write and let things fall where they may. I don't know who the killer is until the end. After all, if I can't guess who the killer is, the readers certainly won't!"

It's a lovely but misguided sentiment that really has nothing to do with structure. You still have to write an ending that satisfies and, if it doesn't, figure out how to make it so.

That's a matter of knowing what structure does. As the great screenwriter and director Billy Wilder once put it, "If you have a problem with the third act, the real problem is in the first act."

Know what the acts do and you can solve a ton of problems in your book.

Which is why I've written Super Structure.

3

How to Use Super Structure

I recently received a nice email from a college freshman, with a great question. In my book, *Write Your Novel From the Middle*, I had a brief mention of my Super Structure beats. My correspondent wrote me this:

> I am reading *Write Your Novel from the Middle*, and I have a question: can a good story be written at the end of the second pillar without Mounting Forces, Lights Out, Q Factor, Final Battle, and Transformation? If it is sort of cut short by defeat, like there could be more where the character fights back against his fate but doesn't? Would that make a good downer, or would it just be bad writing?

What a great and insightful question from someone just starting their writing journey. Here's what I said in reply:

> You touch on a crucially important point: you, the writer and artist, have the ultimate say in how your story turns out and what you want it to mean. Structure is there to guide you and will never let you down. But if you see a path — or your story seems to be urging you to jump into a dark cave — go

exploring. Make the jump and see what happens. You can always come back to structure, which will be waiting for you with open arms.

Never consider anything you try along these lines as "bad writing." It's important that you do not. Your creative self needs running room. Then, after you're out of breath, you can rest a bit and assess what you've done and make informed decisions about it.

Structure is about helping you be more informed.

What you call a "downer" may be another way of describing a tragedy. That's where transformation is possible, and a victory (over self) is being offered, but the Lead declines. In that case structure still works for you by giving the reader a sense that maybe the Lead will indeed make it, but doesn't. The last stage, Transformation, is not realized.

As far as your ending being "cut short," it all depends what you mean. If a reader gets past the "second pillar" and suddenly the confrontation is over because the Lead stops "fighting back against his fate," that may be too much of a jolt. A sudden stop, leaving the reader wondering, "Is that all? It's over? He just stops fighting?"

If that's the feeling you get later on as you read the ending, what do you do? Go back and see if you can fill in more gaps. The Lead going through the various stages at the end, and THEN being defeated might work much better. Structure will, again, guide you.

And just to clarify, writing downer endings is not the issue. Many writers choose those based upon their themes and view of the world. It's HOW you get there that matters most, and structure will help you ... if you want it to!

For you are the ultimate artist. You are the final decision maker. You are also a lifelong student of the craft, if you are really a writer, so let structure be your prof whenever you need it.

Below are some tips on how to be creative and free and get ready for Super Structure to supercharge your novel.

Getting Ready to Write

How does a story begin? I'm not talking about your first page. I'm talking about your *idea,* your spark.

When does the spark start a fire? That's the point where you begin developing story.

This is a wild, exciting wilderness where there are no rules or structures or forms. This is the time when you let go and explode, picking up the pieces later.

But there will come a time for the ordering of your expanding universe.

As the great Dwight Swain says in *Techniques of the Selling Writer,* "Get excited! Hunt until you come to something or other to which you react. With feeling. The more intensely, the better." He's talking here about this initial phase. The inspiration for it can come from anywhere. And it is *feelings based.* This is what the No Rules School thinks should be the whole of writing a novel.

But not Swain. For later on that same page he writes, "*After* you find your feeling, rules come in handy ... help you figure out the best way to capture in words whatever it is that so excites you."

In other words, structure and plotting craft translates your excitements onto the page so readers can share them with you.

Now let me say that "writing by the numbers" is not the bugaboo some people make it out to be. It can certainly be pursued, and profitably. Erle Stanley Gardner, for example, will never be mistaken for a Nobel Prize winner. But he was at one time the bestselling author in the world, writing the Perry Mason novels according to a mystery formula he created for himself.

Gardner used a self-designed "plot wheel" to start him brainstorming a plot. He would work out the intricate plot like a man designing a complex mousetrap. And then he'd write the book in a matter of weeks or days, usually by dictating to a stenographer.

He made a very nice living that way, and someone just as intelligent and enterprising as Gardner might be able to do the same.

My way is in the middle. I like to write thrillers. It's what I love to read. A twisty, turny, actiony plot is my meat.

But I also like great writing. I love sentences that sing. Genre books that attempt to go deeper than their entertaining surface are my preferred reading.

One of my favorite writers is John D. MacDonald, best known today as the creator of Travis McGee. But in the 50s he wrote a string of paperback originals that rank among the best output of that whole era.

I like what he once said about what he looks for in a writer. I call it MacDonald's Credo. Here it is, from the introduction to his collection of stories *The Good Old Stuff*:

First, there has to be a strong sense of story. I want to be intrigued by wondering what is going to happen next. I want the people that I read about to be in difficulties--emotional, moral, spiritual, whatever, and I want to live with them while they're finding their way out of these difficulties.

Second, I want the writer to make me suspend my disbelief. I want to be in some other place and scene of the writer's devising.

Next, I want him to have a bit of magic in his prose style, a bit of unobtrusive poetry. I want to have words and phrases that really sing. And I like an attitude of wryness, realism, the sense of inevitability. I think that writing--good writing-- should be like listening to music, where you identify the themes, you see what the composer is doing with those themes, and then, just when you think you have him properly identified, and his methods identified, then he will put in a little quirk, a little twist, that will be so unexpected that you read it with a sense of glee, a sense of joy, because of its aptness, even though it may be a very dire and bloody part of the book.

So I want story, wit, music, wryness, color, and a sense of reality in what I read, and I try to get it in what I write.

That is a satisfying way to write. For me at least. And maybe it will be for you, too.

To quote Swain once more from his famous book, "Feeling tells you what you want to say. Technique gives you tools with which to say it."

Feel, then, with all your heart. But don't ever think that's going to write you a novel that sells. Technique, of which Super Structure is a part, is just as essential. It's both/and, not either/or.

Remember That Your Novel is About Death

In my writings and talks about structure, I emphasize that the overall plot of a novel is about how a character confronts death.

Unless it's life and death, the stakes aren't high enough.

Now, there are three kinds of death: physical, professional, psychological.

The first kind is the stuff of thrillers. There's usually a bad guy, or group of bad guys, trying to kill a good guy.

The second kind occurs when the job of the Lead is the reason the action takes place. For example, a legal thriller need not involve physical death. It can be about a lawyer taking a case. You, the author, have to make it clear that this case is a matter of the lawyer's very profession. If she loses the case, it will mean her reputation, or ability to practice, or disbarment. Something that important.

This kind of death can also be about a role the character has taken on, or has thrust upon him. In *Kramer v. Kramer*, a hard-working father must suddenly become a presence in his son's life. If he does not fulfill this role successfully, he risks losing custody of his only child. It will be his "death" as a father.

Finally, there is psychological death. The main battle is inside the Lead. The character is on a quest for personhood, for full humanity. If she doesn't make it, it will be like "dying on the inside."

An example is *White Oleander* by Janet Fitch, about a girl thrust into the foster care system. Will she come out permanently damaged, or stronger and more complete?

The Catcher in the Rye is about an adolescent boy's search for authenticity in the world. It's not an idle search. It is made clear by the writing that if Holden Caulfield does not find it he will either have lasting mental problems or, perhaps, even kill himself.

One of these kinds of death should be primary in your novel. You should be able to sum up the main plot of your book with one of the three woven into the summary.

For example, if you were to formulate a summary for the film *The Fugitive*, it would be something like this: *Dr. Richard Kimble, wrongly convicted of murdering his wife, escapes a prison bus and goes on the run. He's got to find some way to elude a national manhunt, because if he is caught he will be executed in the gas chamber.* (Physical death.)

The Verdict is about *an aging, alcoholic lawyer whose ability and means to practice law are about to expire. When he gets a major case that he truly cares about, he knows he has to win it or he will be finished as a real lawyer.* (Professional death.)

You can have more than one kind of death at stake. For instance, in *The Fugitive*, if Kimble does not get justice for his wife, he will certainly die on the inside before he's put into the big sleep. But physical death is primary.

Being able to define the type of death that overhangs your main plot will keep you on track when you write your novel. It will bring you back to the path if you happen to get lost along the way.

Ways to Brainstorm a Story

There are as many ways to brainstorm a story as there are writers. And yet no single one of them is the "right" one. Below are some of my favorite methods. Feel free to adapt them to your own use.

Remember, this is playtime. This is where plotters and pantsers can hold hands and go traipsing through the tulips of imagination together!

The White-Hot Document

This may be my favorite. I learned about it from Dwight Swain, in his classic *Techniques of the Selling Writer.* You simply start writing a doc with whatever comes to mind, jotting down story and character ideas as they come. Write without thinking too much. Let your subconscious throw you whatever it wants to throw you.

Write a lot.

Follow tangents.

Then set the document aside for a day, and come back to it and annotate it. You look it over, find the best parts, highlight things you like, deepen initial thoughts and so on.

Then write hot again, adding more of the bubbling crude from your writer's brain.

Again, come back to it the next day and annotate again. Do this as many times as you like.

David Morrell, in *Lessons From a Lifetime of Writing,* suggests a similar method. He does his free-form document as a series of questions he asks himself. Things like, What interests me about this idea? Why do I want to write this? How can I go deeper?

The point is to get the boys in the basement (Stephen King's wonderful metaphor) working up a sweat and sending you lots of fresh material.

I'll spend four or five days on this document. Then I want to start creating scenes.

Scene Cards

I like to take a stack of fifty or so index cards to my local coffee hangout. I get my brew and sit in a comfortable chair. Then I start imagining scenes. Whatever picture comes into my head.

When something vivid comes to mind, I jot the idea on a card. The notation may be as brief as: *Bar fight with biker.* Or it might have a little more detail: *Chase through Central Market, flinging Chop-Suey at each other.*

I'll do a few of these on the fly, then prompt myself with something from outside my mind. I carry a small dictionary, and will open it at random and find the first noun I see. That word gets fresh pictures dancing in my head, and I use it to create a scene.

When I've got around fifty scene cards, which may take a couple of hours to generate, I shuffle them and pick two at random and see what connections they suggest. That leads to more scenes.

Eventually, I take the best scenes and organize them by which act they naturally fall into.

Then I'll recreate those scenes in digital form on Scrivener. (I'm a Scrivener fan, and suggest that it is especially good for structural organization of a manuscript.)

Elevator Pitch

If you can formulate your idea into a compelling, 30-second pitch, you'll know you have at least a solid base from which to launch into your writing.

I teach an elevator pitch that is three sentences.

The first describes the character, his vocation, and initial circumstances.

The second is the Doorway of No Return (explained in Part II of this book).

The third is the death stakes. So it looks like this:

Dorothy Gale is a farm girl who dreams of getting out of Kansas to a land far, far away, where she and her dog will be safe from the likes of town busybody Miss Gulch.

But when a twister hits the farm, Dorothy is transported to a land of strange creatures and at least one wicked witch who wants to kill her.

Now, with the help of three unlikely friends, Dorothy must find a way to destroy the wicked witch who wants her dead, so the great wizard will send her back home.

Work on your pitch until it becomes like great back-cover copy on a printed book. What would compel a reader to buy?

LOCK System

The first article I had published in *Writer's Digest* explained what I call the LOCK System. It was my earliest attempt to explain the fundamental components of a successful novel, and make them simple and accessible. LOCK stands for: Lead, Objective, Confrontation, and Knockout.

If you nail only those four things, you can write any draft with confidence.

Your first task is to bond your readers with your **Lead.**

Then you give the story the **Objective**, which is to fight with some form of death.

The opposing force is what makes for **Confrontation**.

Finally, there is a titanic battle at the end, inner and/or outer, mental and/or physical. And the result must be an absolute **Knockout** for the reader—which means they are supremely satisfied they bought your book!

Stay Loose

Super Structure is flexible. You don't have to know every scene with specificity beforehand. It's enough to know what type of scene ought to be placed where. This alone can guide you along the path of discovering your true story.

I almost always start with a concept, a "what if?" question. *What if a man had to protect himself and his brother from killers?* That's what triggered my novel *Don't Leave Me.* I wanted to write about a brother relationship in a thriller.

Next, I'll do some character work on the Lead, start to get to know him. And then the other main characters.

I start my white-hot document, as mentioned above.

Then scenes.

Lately, I've started focusing on one scene in particular, the **Mirror Moment** (these terms will all be explained in Part II). I get to this early on, because it illuminates what story is trying to get out. It makes everything else I think up organic and connected.

Once I know the Mirror Moment, I can then plot out the pre-story psychology of the character and know where his arc leads: to the **Transformation** at the end.

Which will also give me the **Argument Against Transformation.**

Next, I'll map out Act I, especially that first **Doorway of No Return**. I'll think about the other signposts, but won't necessarily fill them all in with specifics. Maybe jot some ideas, but that's it.

Then I'm ready for the journey.

Now, on the subject of staying loose, I want to say something very important. These signposts are here to help you, not bonk you over the head. You can certainly use each and every one of them to form a potent outline. But if you are the kind of writer who doesn't like to over-plan, I offer this practical advice—concentrate on the following beats:

Act I
Disturbance
Doorway of No Return #1
Act II
Mirror Moment
Doorway of No Return #2
Act III
Final Battle

THESE FIVE BEATS are the mainstays, the tent poles, the solid supports. If you nail these, you'll have a story. You will also have plenty of freedom to write in between these scenes.

When you need them, the other signposts will be available to help you decide what to write in those gaps—if you want that help.

4

Creativity As You Write

After you have conceived your story and started to map it out (see the previous chapter), you begin the writing phase. Just because you think about structure as you write does not mean you turn off your creative engines.

The art and craft of great fiction comes down to marrying the fire of your creativity with the solidity of structure. Do that, and you'll warm the cockles of your readers' hearts.

Hot cockles sell books.

Here are some ways to stay in creative flow as you write.

The Novel Journal

I got this idea from Sue Grafton, author of the amazing Kinsey Millhone series. As of this writing there are 23 titles, from A - W, in this set. How has Grafton managed it?

One way is by journaling her way through each novel. She begins her writing sessions by noting something personal in the journal. This gives her a picture of what's going on in her own life at that particular time. She may even use some of that material in the current book.

Then she begins by asking herself questions about the work-in-progress. What does this development mean? How can she use it later in the book?

How about this character who has shown up? What will he mean to the plot?

What's the next thing that can happen?

What future scenes need to be in the book?

She thinks all this through in the journal. This is the playground and her workshop.

Then she gets to her daily writing of the project.

Try it. Start your sessions by writing for five minutes in your journal. Go wild, ask questions, and brainstorm answers.

Then write.

The Boys in the Basement

Each night before you nod off, ask your subconscious mind a major question about the story.

As your head hits the pillow, picture the last scene you wrote. Vividly. Then let your mind suggest other pictures, things that might happen later on.

Go to sleep.

Have your phone or tablet on your bed table, or at least paper and pen, so you can memorialize any flashes of genius that wake you up.

Second thing in the morning (after starting the coffee) write for five intense minutes. Write anything that comes to mind. Write your impressions, visions, dreams, ideas.

Have your coffee.

Then try to figure out what your boys in the basement are trying to say to you. Pick out the best ideas and use them in your novel.

Exercise

When you get tired after a writing stint, try a little exercise. The pumping of blood and endorphins stimulates the creative state.

Another thing you can do is write in 25 minute segments. Time them. Then walk around for 5 - 10 minutes. Or lie on the floor with your feet up on a chair and deep breathe for 10 minutes. This is the true pause that refreshes.

Mind Map

Every now and then take a sheet of blank paper and do a mind map of your story. Write the names of your characters in little bubbles around the page. Then make links to story events or other characters.

There's something about using a pen across paper that gets another part of the brain going.

Let's not put the pen manufacturers out of business.

Skip Ahead

If you ever get bogged down in a scene, put a little marker there and skip ahead. Write the next thing that excites you. Go back and fill in the gaps later.

ALL THIS IS CREATIVE FLOW. It's a good thing. But it's not the only thing.

You must channel it into something awesomely coherent.

That's what Super Structure is for.

5

The Structure of Scenes

"The fictional scene is the way the story happens. It is also the way the reader experiences the novel or story. In its pure essence, a work of fiction is a sequence of scenes from page one to the end. But life does not come to us packaged in a series of scenes. It is up to the writer to package it." — William Sloane *The Craft of Writing*

Before we launch into the secrets of Super Structure in the next part of this book, I want to talk for a moment about scenes. Scenes are the building blocks of fiction. You can't have a novel without scenes. And you can't write great scenes without structure.

Why is that?

Because you need *conflict*.

Conflict doesn't just happen. You have to *make* it happen.

Not only that, you have to make it clear to the reader who the players are and what is at stake for them in the scene.

A scene has the following elements:

Objective

Each scene must have a scene objective. That is, from whatever POV you're in, there must be a moving force in the scene, trying to make something happen.

- A cop is questioning a witness, trying to get information.
- A mother who has lost a child is trying to forget her pain.
- A Navy SEAL is trying to kill five assassins at once.
- A man is drinking to keep from confronting the fact that he's cheated on his wife.

The reader needs to know what the POV character wants in a scene. Even if he's alone, the character needs to want something: comfort, quiet, a cool drink.

The objective can be explicit:

"Man, I need a cool drink," he said.

Or made clear through the action.

He got up and went into the kitchen, opened the refrigerator, looked for a beer.

Opposition

What person, place, thing or circumstance is keeping the POV character from gaining the objective?

- The witness is lying to the cop, and even has a gun.
- The mother keeps seeing her missing child in every object in the house.
- Assassins are good at what they do. That's why they're assassins.
- Alcohol dulls, but doesn't destroy the conscience.

As you can see, the opposition element can be outer (as in another character) or inner (as in the character's psychology and thought patterns).

Further, you can have social opposition. Any group of people who have an interest in the status quo can provide this. For instance, Rick Dadier in Evan Hunter's *The Blackboard Jungle* is a teacher who thinks he can make a difference in a tough school. Most of the other teachers, and administration, don't think so. This makes for several tense scenes in the book and movie.

Finally, nature itself can provide opposition in a scene. It can provide the basic opposition for an entire novel or script, as in Stephen King's *Storm of the Century*. Don't ever get stuck on an island off the coast of Maine in winter if King is writing the story. He's liable to drop a pathological killer in there.

Nature or circumstance can be a great obstacle when time is of the essence. The character needs to get to town, but the bridge is out. Or a storm puts a tree across the road. Or the car itself breaks down.

The nice thing about being an author is you get to choose.

Outcome

Each scene has to end at some point. In general a scene can end:

1. Well.
2. Not so well.
3. Terribly.

In the realm of fiction, the worse the scene ends, either overtly or implicitly, the better.

Because people read to worry. They want to watch a Lead they're bonded with go through the trials and tribulations of the story. The more success, the less worry.

Design your scenes so, for the most part, the Lead is in a worse position after the scene is over.

- She doesn't get the information she wants.
- Worse, she gets some information that hurts her.
- Worse still, she is knocked out by a hammer.

There is an infinite variety of bad outcomes to choose from.

This does not mean that a scene cannot end well. Occasionally, for breathing space, have something good happen.

But use that good to lead to something bad.

Or to portend more trouble.

Something Unexpected

Further, a great scene will have something unexpected.

This can be a plot twist, a new character, a fresh description, even a line of dialogue. Anything that throws a reader's expectations off is a good thing.

So how do you find those unexpected gems?

You brainstorm for five minutes before you write the scene.

Write down the POV character in the scene, the objective, and a list of possible obstacles. Write a tentative outcome.

Spend a couple of minutes making a list of unexpected things. Go wild. One of them will please you.

Then you're ready to write.

Did you hear that? Ready to write! Let's get on with it. Let's dive into the powerful, unleashing secrets of Super Structure. Understand what these beats actually do, and why. I'll tell you. I'll even give you hints on how to use them, be ye plotter or pantser or something in between.

The point is it's all for your benefit, and you can decide how to use it.

6

Emotional Structure

A common knock on structure is that it leads to by-the-numbers writing with no blood in its veins.

Wrong.

It's not the fault of structure.

It's the fault of by-the-numbers writers with no blood in their veins.

The answer, then, is not to ditch structure.

It's to get blood pumping in the *writer,* and then in the characters. That's the progression.

There are many ways to approach emotional structure. Mine is to golf it.

I'd better explain.

When I was first learning to golf I followed the same plan I used when learning how to write.

I read books and practiced what I learned.

I had a few teachers watch me and critique me and improve me.

I played as much as I could.

Gradually, I got to a very good point in my golf game: not embarrassing myself. It was fun to be able to go out with anyone on any course and not keep the party behind us waiting while I took several hacks at a ball in the rough.

It's also a great feeling when you reach this point in your writing. You can get there, if you study and practice.

One of the big lessons I picked up was from a golf video on the mental part of the game. What goes on between the ears is just as important, sometimes more so, than what goes on with the hands.

A sports psychologist counseled a simple routine before a swing:

See it.

Feel it.

Trust it.

In other words, visualize the shot you want to make. Let that image pour into your muscles. Then forget everything else but trusting what you feel.

Only after the round is over do you think about any mistakes or mechanics, and try to fix them.

I think this is the perfect method for structuring the emotions in your novel, too.

See it

When you are about to write a scene, take a moment to play it in the movie theater of your mind. Watch the scene unfold. Let the characters improvise.

Watch until you feel something.

You will.

Feel it

Drink in the feeling.

Many writers, myself included, use music to enhance emotion. I like movie soundtracks for this. I have a large library and have separated the songs into "mood lists."

When I'm writing suspense, I'll put on my suspense list, which is heavily populated by the Bernard Herrmann scores of Alfred Hitchcock movies.

For poignant scenes, I have the score to my favorite movie, *The Best Years of Our Lives* and others like it, such as *A River Runs Through It* and *The Road to Perdition*.

If I need inspiration and heroics, there's *Rudy* and *The Big Country*.

And if I need energy to write, I've got classic Rock. There's nothing quite like Elliott Randall's guitar solo in Steely Dan's *Reelin' in the Years* to get you writing again.

Trust it

Now, write the scene. Don't think. Trust.

Keep feeling as you write.

Go off on an emotional tear if it feels right to you. Sometimes I'll open up a text-only doc and just write for five minutes on the emotions and inner thoughts of the POV character. I always find two or three lines I can use in the actual scene. But I never would have found them at all if I hadn't taken that five-minute tangent.

When in doubt, *overwrite* the emotions. Let 'em rip. Heat is better than tepid. You can always dial it back later, when you revise. But first time out, go for it.

Fix it

When you revise your scene or manuscript, that's the time to analyze the emotional structure and render it in the most effective way.

Ask yourself:

- Does the emotion feel right?
- Is it consistent with the character?

- Does it reveal a new side of the character?
- Does it enhance the scene?
- Does it contribute to the overall plot?

Next, look at *how* you have given us the emotions. There are generally five ways to render emotion on the page.

1. You can name it
2. You can show it through action
3. You can show it through physical reaction
4. You can show it through internal thoughts
5. You can show it through dialogue

Number one, naming it, is best reserved for low intensity parts of a scene. Let's say a mother has come home from the grocery store and is about to find out that her thirteen-year-old daughter is not in her room, where she ought to be doing her homework. And then she will find a ransom note.

Obviously, this scene builds in intensity.

When she first comes in the house, what is her emotion? Maybe she had a run-in with a jerk in the parking lot who almost hit her.

You might simply write, *Still annoyed with that jerk from the parking lot, Janet set the bags on her kitchen counter.* Why this? Because if you attempt to *show* every emotion, you will wear the reader out. There's no need for it. Sometimes you name an emotion to set the stage.

But as soon as a scene begins to heat up, consider the other four ways of showing emotion.

You can use them any way you choose, giving you an infinite palette of possibilities.

To help you in this, let me recommend the book *The Emotion Thesaurus* by Angela Ackerman and Becca Puglisi. It's a compendium of ways to show emotion and can be of enormous help when the time comes to turn up the heat.

In sum, structure helps you determine what kind of scene to write. The emotion you pack into it deepens the reading experience.

You'll be writing on all cylinders now.

You're ready for the journey to begin.

That journey is the subject of the rest of this book.

PART II

The Fourteen Signposts

Remember, Super Structure is here to help you, not slap you around. As I mentioned earlier, the five "tent poles" of structure are: Disturbance, Doorway of No Return #1, Mirror Moment, Doorway of No Return #2, and Final Battle.

The other signposts fall into an organic pattern. Feel free to use them all to map out your book, or wait until you need a suggestion.

Here is their natural progression:

Act I (no greater than 20% of your novel)

1. Disturbance
2. Care Package
3. Argument against Transformation
4. Trouble Brewing
5. Doorway of No Return #1

Act II (that large middle portion where the main action takes place)

6. Kick in the Shins
7. The Mirror Moment
8. Pet the Dog

9. Doorway of No Return #2

Act III (the resolution)

10. Mounting Forces

11. Lights Out

12. Q Factor

13. Final Battle

14. Transformation

That's not too much to think about, is it? That's not an iron fist beating the creativity out of you.

In fact it will gently guide your creativity in the right directions, giving you the best shot at connecting with readers.

Connection with readers = sales.

If you're interested in selling your fiction, that's the formula for success.

"But I don't want to write to a formula!"

Please re-read Chapter 2.

Then start your engines on the road to Super Structure. You see that first signpost up ahead? That's where your story begins.

It's called The Disturbance.

1

Disturbance

What is the opening shot, after the credits, in *The Wizard of Oz?*

Go ahead and think of your answer.

When I ask this question in workshops, I get various answers. The most popular is, "The lady on the bicycle."

Nope, she's not till later.

Surprisingly, some say it's the cyclone. But of course that isn't until we're almost a quarter of the way into the movie.

What did you come up with?

The correct answer is a shot of a dirt road in rural Kansas with a girl running away from something. She has her dog with her. She looks back over her shoulder.

Clearly, she's frightened.

But we don't know why.

What we *do* know is that she is experiencing a big disturbance to her ordinary world.

It's precisely the right way to start a story.

The great spy novelist John Le Carré suggested this axiom: The cat sat on the mat is not the beginning of a story. The cat sat on the dog's mat, is.

Another writer said that a story begins when you strike the match, not when you lay out the wood.

I see way too many manuscripts that are of the wood-prep variety.

Why is that?

I call it the Happy People in Happy Land Fallacy.

This kind of manuscript begins with a chapter that has no conflict or trouble. The opening scene depicts a lead character who is very nice, living in a nice world. Maybe she's a mother with a happy family. Maybe he's a man with a good job and future.

And they are going through their ordinary day, delighted as can be, being nice to people.

The strategy, in the minds of the writers, is to make us care for these wonderful folks, so when the trouble really starts we'll be rooting for them.

The problem is the scene is too boring to hold our interest.

Because what hooks a reader to a character is not how nice they are, *but what trouble, challenge, or change threatens them.*

These days, when more and more readers decide to buy a book based on the free sampling of the opening pages, you simply can't afford to bore them.

You need to make trouble.

Trouble is your friend.

Trouble is your business.

So start your business immediately with some sort of disturbance.

From the first paragraph, or even the first line.

Let me give you a few examples.

In Chapter 1 of Stephenie Meyer's *Twilight*, teenage Bella moves to a small town and is immediately thrust into a new school. This is always disturbing. No friends, no history. We naturally identify with this, because we're human and we've all been through something similar.

The first line is: *My mother drove me to the airport with the windows rolled down.* By the end of the paragraph we know this is a farewell. That's change.

And change is a type of disturbance.

You can also *allude* to trouble yet to come, as Dean Koontz does in *Fear Nothing:*

> On the desk in my candlelit study, the telephone rang, and I knew that a terrible change was coming.

Or to a disturbance that's already happened, and will be explained, as in Lawrence Block's *Ariel:*

> Was there a noise that woke her? Roberta was never sure.

You can always use an intriguing first line:

> I feel compelled to report that at the moment of death, my entire life did not pass before my eyes in a flash. (*"I" is for Innocent,* Sue Grafton)

> The first time my husband hit me I was nineteen years old. (*Black and Blue*, Anna Quindlen)

> When the sixth floor of the Las Palmas Hotel caught fire Robbie Brownlaw was in the diner across the street about to have lunch. (*The Fallen*, T. Jefferson Parker)

> "Do your neighbors burn one another alive?" was how Fraa Orolo began his conversation with Artisan Flec. (*Anathem*, Neal Stephenson)

You can place the disturbance at the end of your first paragraph, too, providing a "jolt" factor. Here is the opening of *The Day After Tomorrow* by Allan Folsom:

> Paul Osborn sat alone among the smoky bustle of the after-work crowd, staring into a glass of red wine. He was tired and

hurt and confused. For no particular reason he looked up. When he did, his breath left him with a jolt. Across the room sat the man who murdered his father.

Harlan Coben uses one, long sentence with a jolt at the end in the opening of *Promise Me:*

> The missing girl – there had been unceasing news reports, always flashing to that achingly ordinary school portrait of the vanished teen, you know the one, with the rainbow–swirl background, the girl's hair too straight, her smile too self–conscious, then a quick cut to the worried parents on the front lawn, microphones surrounding them, Mom silently tearful, Dad reading a statement with quivering lip – that girl, that missing girl, had just walked past Edna Skylar.

More first lines from Mr. Koontz:

> Penny Dawson woke and heard something moving furtively in the dark bedroom. (*Darkfall*)

> Katharine Sellers was sure that, at any moment, the car would begin to slide along the smooth, icy pavement and she would lose control of it. (*Dance With the Devil*, written as "Deanna Dwyer")

> Tuesday was a fine California day, full of sunshine and promise, until Harry Lyon had to shoot someone at lunch. (*Dragon Tears*)

A "literary" novel (which is often defined as less about plot and more about character) still needs a disturbing start. Anne Lamott provides one in *Blue Shoe:*

The world outside the window was in flames. The leaves on the pistachio trees shone fire-red and orange. Mattie studied the early morning light. She was lying on the side of the bed where her husband should have been sleeping.

See how subtle it is, but still disturbing? Where is her husband? Is he merely in the kitchen making coffee? Or is he dead? Or has he left her?

We read to find out. There is plenty of time to fill in essential information.

Why This Works

The opening of your book is often the make-or-break part of the sale.

If an agent or editor or reader sees a slow opening, one that does not engage, the obstacle to selling the book goes up exponentially.

Why take that chance?

The Disturbance works because it is about trouble.

Trouble is the lifeblood of fiction.

Helpful Hints for Plotters and Pantsers

Write several opening lines. Often it's not the first one you write, but the fifth or sixth that really grabs you. And if it grabs you it will grab the reader.

Include opening with two character in a tense dialogue exchange. Immediate conflict is trouble for someone, and that's always a good thing for your fiction.

Super Structure Reminder

Disturbances don't have to happen just at the beginning. You can sprinkle them throughout. When in doubt about what to write next, make more trouble. Raymond Chandler used to say, just bring in a guy with a gun. You can create the same feeling in a variety of ways, consistent with your genre.

2

Care Package

My thriller, *Don't Leave Me*, is the story of the bond between two brothers. Chuck Samson, an ex-Navy chaplain who served with a Marine unit in Afghanistan, and his adult, autistic brother, Stan, who has a heart as big as the Pacific. And what happens when killers come after them both.

Chuck, who is suffering from PTSD, finds his solace in the fifth graders he teaches at a private school. He loves those kids, especially the ones who don't quite fit in.

I bring this up because these two examples, Stan and the kids, are examples of what I call the Care Package. It is a story element that greatly enhances reader connection to the Lead.

The Care Package is a relationship the Lead has with someone else, in which he shows his concern, through word or deed, for that character's well being.

This humanizes the Lead and engenders sympathy in the reader. It works even if the Lead happens to be a louse, because this one element gives the reader hope that the Lead might be redeemed.

Let me give you a few examples of the Care Package in action.

In *The Hunger Games*, Katniss Everdeen is not just some lone rogue or anti-hero. She is the protector of and provider for her mother and sister, Prim. What she does in taking Prim's place in the Games is the ultimate sacrifice of love. When she volunteers in place of Prim, we are so much on Katniss' side that we will follow her anywhere, rooting for her all the way.

In *Star Wars,* the only reason Luke will not leave on an adventure with Obi-Wan Kenobe is that his aunt and uncle need him on the farm. Here's a boy who dreams of becoming a knight, but he can't just leave his family. He cares about them, has a duty to them. We like that. It demonstrates nobility.

Soon, of course, his aunt and uncle are murdered ... and Luke is off to fight the evil Empire. We are solidly on his side.

Dorothy Gale cares about Toto in *The Wizard of Oz.* She'll do anything to protect her innocent dog from the clutches of Miss Gulch.

Having a Care Package relationship keeps a character from being completely selfish. We don't like such folk. We hope that we are not that way ourselves.

Scarlett O'Hara, for all her dithering selfishness, cares about her mother and father.

Mike Hammer, not the softest of PIs, cares about his secretary, Velma.

Even the bitter and bigoted Walt Kowalski (Clint Eastwood) in *Gran Torino* cares ... about his dead wife. It is only because of her final wishes that he even tolerates the young priest who keeps showing up to check on him.

The Care Package is one of the reasons we watched *Breaking Bad.* Walter White engages in a truly despicable act — cooking super crystal meth for sale on the street. Yet he holds some degree of sympathy. He gets into the trade because he's dying of cancer and wants to provide for his wife and handicapped son.

But as the story progresses, Walter becomes more ruthless and drags his former student, Jesse, into this dark world.

And yet ... and yet ... whenever Jesse gets in real trouble, Walt tries to get him out of it. He *cares* about Jesse in spite of all that happens. And Jesse cares about Mr. White. They forget about this caring at various times when they want to kill each other, but it always comes back when the chips are down.

Now that is good writing, and a great lesson. You can have a criminal as your Lead, and if you give him a Care Package, you'll still tug on the emotional strings of the reader.

In my workshops on structure I stress the difference between the Care Package and the later beat called Pet the Dog. The latter is something that happens in Act II, when the Lead takes a moment out of her own troubles to help someone weaker than herself.

The Care Package, by contrast, is a relationship the Lead has *before* the story begins. Thus, sometime early in Act I, we are given a glimpse of this bond.

Why This Works

A novel's primary effect should be emotional. Please review the chapter on Emotional Structure.

It does not matter if you have a message you want to send or a twisty plot idea. Unless the reader experiences the narrative on an emotional level — and this from the start — the chances of your book being set aside increase.

The Care Package is one structural move that reduces those odds.

Helpful Hints for Plotters and Pantsers

You plotters/outliners might consider using a Care Package as the emotional starting point for your developing story. That's what I did with *Don't Leave Me*. I got the initial idea of writing about a former military chaplain. I started to think about his backstory, and almost immediately came up with the idea of his having an autistic brother he has protected all of their lives, and now must do again when killers arrive on the scene.

It was such a strong emotional tie for me that it incentivized my wanting to write the entire novel, just to vindicate this relationship.

Pantsers, as you are writing along, maybe 10,000 words into that wonderful mess you love, why not pause for a moment and consider the main character who is starting to come to life? You don't have to worry about structure here, just ask yourself what kind of relationship can the Lead have with someone else that shows a caring spirit?

Heck, you're a pantser! Go ahead and write a scene like that. The benefit to you is a greater emotional connection that you, the author, have with your Lead. And that's going to make for a better book.

Super Structure Reminder

When you show a character's humanity, you link her up to the collective unconscious of the audience. Don't be afraid to show humanity: caring, flaws, foibles, doubts, inner conflict, love, passion, anger, frailty as well as strength.

3

Argument Against
Transformation

This is a very cool beat I picked up from watching and analyzing many classic films. You don't always see it, but when you do it is a terrific way of framing the character arc in a story.

The easiest way to explain it is to start with the idea of theme. What is the theme of a novel? How is it stated?

Writing teachers have different ideas about it, but my formulation is that it's about a "life lesson learned." What is it that the character learns by the end of the story? What truth is it that she will live by from then on?

Everybody knows the lesson in *The Wizard of Oz*. *There's no place like home.* Dorothy had to learn that the hard way.

But early in the film, in the very first scene, in fact, Dorothy argues against this notion. She's run back to the farm and everyone is ignoring her cry for help about Miss Gulch and her desire to snuff Toto.

Aunt Em tells Dorothy to stop imagining things, and find a herself a place where she won't get into any trouble.

Dorothy takes Toto aside and muses on that. "Some place where there isn't any trouble. Do you suppose there is such a place, Toto? There must be. It's not a place you can get to by a boat or a train. It's far, far away, behind the moon, beyond the rain ... somewhere over the rainbow ..."

This sets up the character arc in the reader's mind. When she learns the real lesson at the end, the arc has closed, the inner problem has been solved.

In *Casablanca*, Rick begins by telling people, "I stick my neck out for nobody." He proves that as the helpless Ugarte screams at Rick to help him escape the French police, about to arrest him for murdering two German couriers.

Even as Ugarte is dragged out, Rick lifts not a finger. Another of his customers expresses the wish that when the police come for him Rick will be a little more helpful. Rick merely states his code once more: "I stick my neck out for nobody."

And what does he learn at the end? That there are times when it is right not only to stick out your neck for someone, but to sacrifice your happiness and even life for them. That's what he does when he gives up his chance to flee Casablanca with his great love, Ilsa.

The arc has closed.

In *It's a Wonderful Life*, what is the life lesson learned? It's that no man is a failure if he stays in his own home town and lives a life helping his neighbors. But that's not what the young George Bailey thinks.

As a boy working in the drug store, he tells the two girls—Mary and Violet—that when he grows up he's going on adventures. He's going to have "a couple of harems, and maybe three or four wives. Wait and see."

He is arguing against the transformation that will take place by the end.

There's a great argument against transformation in my favorite action film, *Lethal Weapon*. Riggs (Mel Gibson) is the suicidal cop. His wife was murdered so he doesn't care if he gets shot in the line of duty. Indeed, he longs for it.

After getting a jumper off a roof in a most unorthodox fashion, his partner, Murtaugh (Danny Glover) pulls him aside and screams at him. "Do you want to die?"

Riggs screams back at him. Yes he wants to die! He thinks all the time about eating a bullet. Riggs pulls out a hollow point that he carries around with him, holds it up, says this will blow the back of his head off. He tells Murtaugh he has to think of a reason not to do it, every day! And the only reason he doesn't is "the job."

There is no reason to go on living except the job, and even that seems tenuous at best.

That's his argument.

Does he transform at the end? Indeed, and with a marvelous visual. See the chapter on Transformation for that.

In *To Kill a Mockingbird*, the lesson Scout must learn is empathy for people who are different from her, even those her society regards with scorn.

Scout argues against this in Chapter 3 when the poor boy, Walter Cunningham, is a guest for dinner. He makes a poor boy's move by pouring syrup all over his food, meat and vegetables and all. This shocks Scout, who asks what in the Sam Hill he's doing. Walter is duly embarrassed.

The Finch's cook and housekeeper, Calpurnia, demands Scout come out to the kitchen. She lays down the law:

> "There's some folks who don't eat like us," she whispered fiercely, "but you ain't called on to contradict 'em at the table when they don't. That boy's yo' comp'ny and if he wants to eat up the table cloth you let him, you hear?"

Scout then offers up her argument against transformation:

> "He ain't company, Cal, he's just a Cunningham—"

Of course, by the end, Scout has learned the life lesson that we must see things from other people's points of view. We must,

Atticus later explains, "climb into his skin and walk around in it."

In the *Hunger Games* trilogy, there is a great character arc. [If you don't want a spoiler, skip the next few paragraphs.]

The arc is Katniss growing from no hope to hope, from someone who sees no good future to someone prepared to fight for a good future.

Her argument against transformation occurs early in Chapter 1. It's only one line.

"I never want to have kids," I say.

That's the ultimate argument against hope. So what happens at the end of Book 3? She is having a child.

She has been transformed.

Why This Works

Readers, subconsciously, think in arcs. They anticipate completeness, a journey with an end point, a tying up of loose threads. Stories don't always end up this neat and clean, and on occasion an author may choose not to complete the arc. Usually this happens in short stories and literary fiction.

Writing genre fiction is a different matter. Readers expect to be taken on a ride with a definite beginning, middle, and end, and have it mean something when it's over.

You can have a negative arc, too. Michael Corleone in *The Godfather* is an example. In the opening scene he tells his fiancé, Kay, that his family's criminal dealings will not be his life. At the end, he has become the head criminal, and lies to Kay's face about it. He's been transformed all right, but not in a good way.

Helpful Hints for Plotters and Pantsers

If you're a pantser, pause at any time during your writing and take a short break. Grab a cup of joe or do something fun.

Now, come back to your keyboard and write a free-form

document, in the Lead character's voice, explaining to you all the reasons she *should not* be involved in this story. Let it flow. Let the argument happen.

You plotters can start with an Argument Against Transformation as the jumping off point for the rest of your planning. Try it when doing work on your Lead. Do an interview with the character, asking her to expound on her philosophy of life. Let her speak her mind until something clicks.

Place this beat in an early scene in your book.

Super Structure Reminder

Your Lead is not just an action machine. She has beliefs, and those beliefs get challenged by the story events.

4

Trouble Brewing

Somewhere around the middle of Act I is a scene where we get a whiff of big trouble to come. It's not the major conflict yet, because we're not in Act II yet. But we can sense that it's out there, brewing.

It's sort of like a portent. It's not the trouble itself, but a sense of it.

Think of an old sailor standing at the bow of a whaling ship in 1850. He's smoking his pipe and looking out at sea. He feels the wind shift. He takes his pipe out of his mouth and frowns.

The cabin boy asks him if something's wrong.

"Aye, boy, there be a change in the wind."

"What's it mean?" asks the boy.

'There be foul weather ahead, lad. Mighty foul."

That's a portent of trouble.

In *To Kill a Mockingbird,* the narrator, Scout, is going to have some hard lessons to learn about life and prejudice and those who are different. On the very first page we learn about this mysterious person named Boo Radley. His ghostly presence haunts the novel.

In Chapter 4, Scout gets inside a tire and is given a hearty push by her brother Jem. She rolls and rolls, coming to a stop right at the steps of the Radley house. She runs away from there right quick.

The chapter ends this way:

> Atticus's arrival was the second reason I wanted to quit the game. The first reason happened the day I rolled into the Radley front yard. Through all the head-shaking, quelling of nausea and Jem-yelling, I had heard another sound, so low I could not have heard it from the sidewalk. Someone inside the house was laughing.

Trouble brewing, in the form of a mysterious sound. This happens before Chapter 9, which is the first Doorway of No Return for Scout.

In *Gone with the Wind,* Scarlett wants to marry Ashley. Ashley is going to marry Melanie. But that's not it for Scarlett. She waylays Ashley at the big barbecue at Twelve Oaks, coaxing him into the library.

There she cajoles, emotes, insults, and does just about everything else to get Ashley to admit he loves her and not Melanie. Ashley is close to breaking, but his Southern code won't let him. Scarlett slaps him across the face. Ashley walks out. There's trouble brewing, because we know she's not going to let Ashley go without a fight.

But the scene is not over. Scarlett, thinking she's alone, throws a bowl at the fireplace. It shatters.

Which brings Rhett Butler up from the sofa where he'd been lounging, unseen.

Scarlett is aghast. Rhett is amused. And here is another bit of trouble brewing—Rhett Butler is going to complicate her life and her dreams.

This is trouble brewing in the romantic life of Scarlett.

But the main plot development in *GWTW* is the outbreak of the Civil War. That is what throws everyone into crisis mode, and leads to all of the complications.

And in that barbecue scene, all the men can talk about is impending war. They know trouble is coming.

And it does.

Why This Works

After the opening Disturbance, there is a chance to introduce main and minor characters. You have space to set the players in motion, describe the ordinary world, establish the tone of the book and so on. Micro conflict and tension should be present, meaning between the characters But a Trouble Brewing moment reminds the reader that there is bigger conflict to come.

Helpful Hints for Plotters and Pantsers

Often the trouble that brews is in the form of surprising information. In *Lethal Weapon*, Detective Murtaugh, who is investigating the death of a beautiful girl who threw herself off a high-rise building, finds out she is the daughter of an old war buddy of his. This deepens the case.

So in your planning or pantsing, brainstorm bits of information that might be delivered as a surprise.

Another way to get this beat is by thinking of what your villain is doing and planning while "off scene." Something he does can ripple into the "on scene" moment and create the Trouble Brewing beat.

Super Structure Reminder

The "off scene" exercise is great at any point in your writing or planning. When you don't know what to write next, spend some time brainstorming what the other major characters are up to, unseen.

5

Doorway of No Return #1

The beginning of a novel tells us who the main characters are and the situation at hand. It sets us in the story world with a disturbance up front and some hint of the major trouble yet to come. It has conflict and tension, because that's needed for all good scenes.

But the novel does not become "the story" until we get into the confrontation of Act II.

And to get there, the Lead must pass through a Doorway of No Return. The feeling must be that your Lead, once she is across the threshold, cannot go home again. The door slams shut. She has to confront death (physical, professional or psychological) and overcome it, or she will die.

Let's take *Gone with the Wind* as our example.

In the first act, Scarlett O'Hara is sitting on her porch flirting with Brent and Stuart Tarleton. We get to know her as a selfish, scheming, privileged antebellum coquette. She is able to use her charms to enrapture the men around her and play them like carp on a hook. The mother of the Tarleton twins says Scarlett is "a fast piece if ever I saw one."

Now, if this novel were a thousand pages of Scarlett's flirtatious ways, we'd never make it past page ten. A successful novel is about *high stakes trouble*. True character is only revealed in crisis, so Margaret Mitchell gives us some opening trouble (i.e., The Disturbance)—Scarlett learns that Ashley is going to marry Melanie!

That trouble might be enough for a category romance, but not for a sprawling epic of the Old South. There must be something that forces Scarlett into a fight for her very way of life, and that's what the first Doorway is about: it thrusts Scarlett into Act II.

That event is, of course, the outbreak of the Civil War.

On page 127 of my paperback edition of *Gone with the Wind*, Charles Hamilton hastens to Scarlett at the big barbecue at Twelve Oaks:

> "Have you heard? Paul Wilson just rode over from Jonesboro with the news!"
>
> He paused, breathless, as he came up to her. She said nothing and only stared at him.
>
> "Mr. Lincoln has called for men, soldiers—I mean volunteers—seventy-five thousand of them!"

The South sees this as provocation. Charles tells Scarlett it will mean fighting. "But don't you fret, Miss Scarlett, it'll be over in a month and we'll have them howling."

The Civil War is a shattering occurrence Scarlett cannot ignore or wish away. She would rather stay in the Old South and somehow live happily ever after with Ashley.

In mythic terms, Scarlett would like to remain in the "ordinary world." But the outbreak of war *forces* Scarlett into the "dark world" of Act II.

That's why I call this the Doorway of *No Return*. There is no way back to the old, comfortable ways. Scarlett has to face major troubles now. Not just about matters of the heart. She also needs to save her family and her land. She will need money and cleverness.

Act II is where the death stakes are confirmed. For Scarlett, it's psychological death (though her life is in danger at various points). If she doesn't preserve Tara and her vision of the Old South, she will die on the inside. *Gone with the Wind*'s story question is: will Scarlett grow from her old, petty self to the strong self she needs to be? She doesn't want this fight. But she is pushed into it because of the war.

Other examples of the first Doorway of No Return:

In *The Silence of the Lambs* Clarice Starling is thrust into a cat-and-mouse game with Hannibal Lecter because it might be the only way to solve a serial killer case. The novel is about professional death. If young trainee Starling cannot work Lecter as much as he's working her, another victim will die and Starling's career will be over.

In a detective novel, the first Doorway is usually when the detective takes on a client, as Sam Spade does with Brigid O'Shaughnessy in *The Maltese Falcon*. Professional death. The PI *must* solve the mystery because, simply, that's what he does for a living. No solving, no living.

In *To Kill a Mockingbird,* Atticus Finch accepts the job of defending a black man accused of raping a white girl. For Scout Finch, the narrator, this event thrusts her into a dark world of prejudice and injustice. Which way will she go? Will she grow up just like her prejudiced neighbors? If she does, she will have died psychologically.

The timing of the first Doorway should be before the 1/5 mark of your book. In movies, it's common to divide the acts into a 1/4 - 1/2 - 1/4 structure. But in novels it's better to have Doorway #1 happen sooner.

Gone with the Wind is over 1000 pages. The Civil War breaks out at about the 1/10 mark.

In a fast moving action novel like *The Hunger Games* it can happen very early. It's at the beginning of Chapter 3. And it's a literal door. Katniss has just claimed the right to take her sister's place in the games. The anthem of Panem is played and the two tributes of District 12 — Katniss Everdeen and Peter Mellark — are taken into custody.

> I don't mean we're handcuffed or anything, but a group of Peacekeepers marches us through the front door of the Justice Building. Maybe tributes have tried to escape in the past. I've never seen that happen though.

Why This Works

Remember the natural flow of the three acts? If you spend too long in Act I, the story starts to drag. Readers sense it without analysis. They feel it, that the tale has got to kick into high gear before about the 1/5 mark. This Doorway gives a clear demarcation point and a definite passage into the death stakes.

Helpful Hints for Plotters and Pantsers

- Have you given us a character worth following?
- Have you created a disturbance in the opening pages?
- Do you know the death stakes of the story?
- Have you created a scene that will force the character into the confrontation of Act II?
- Is it strong enough? Can the Lead character resist going into the battle?
- Does it occur before the 1/5 mark of your total page count?

Super Structure Reminder

Another way to describe a novel is that it is about a character who confronts challenges by *strength of will*. If the character takes no action, she's just being a wimp. Your Lead must never be a wimp! But sometimes things happen that are out of her control, and feel like a door is slamming behind her, as if in a haunted house. Think of these events as *plot thrust*.

6

Kick in the Shins

Soon after passing through the Doorway of No Return #1, the character must face an obstacle, the first real test in the death stakes of Act II.

This new trouble will be related to the overall story. It is the first challenge to the Lead stepping out into the major confrontation.

Don't wait long for this scene. The reader knows you're now in the heart of things. If you delay the Kick in the Shins too long, the reader begins to wonder if things are really that bad after all.

Let's look at some examples.

The major complicating factor for Scarlett O'Hara's attempt to save Tara and snag Ashley is Rhett Butler. When she met him back in Act I, he'd been lounging in the library when Scarlett had her tantrum with Ashley.

A lot happened after that. Like, the Civil War breaking out. Scarlett marrying Charles Hamilton to spite Ashley. Charles dying of pneumonia.

Now Scarlett, aged sixteen, is a widow (and, in the book, a mother).

In this sad state she goes off to Atlanta to live with relatives.

There she spends a year in mourning, not having any fun, not flirting, not going to parities. Dullsville.

All this time is covered in quick, narrative fashion by Margaret Mitchell.

Finally, Scarlett gets the chance to go to a party! But not to have fun. She will just sit in a booth at a big Atlanta fundraiser for the troops. But at least she'll be *near* music and dancing and fun. She'll take it!

But then who shows up? Rhett Butler!

She's terribly embarrassed. He teases her. She snaps at him.

This is not just another passing moment. Mitchell makes it a Kick in the Shins. The kick happens when Rhett bids a hundred and fifty dollars — in gold! — for Scarlett to dance with him.

Dr. Meade, the emcee, says she cannot do it, for she is in mourning. But Scarlett jumps to her feet. "Yes, I will!"

And so they dance. And Rhett begins his pursuit of Scarlett O'Hara. It's a Kick in the Shins because Scarlett still wants Ashley. Rhett is going to be a complicating factor indeed!

A Kick in the Shins can also be an emotional jolt, a deepening of the interior stakes. That's what happens in *The Hunger Games*.

Recall that Katniss is thrust through the Doorway of No Return #1—*a group of Peacekeepers marches us through the front door of the Justice Building*. Now there is no way out, no escape. She must go forward to the Games.

And what will be a major obstacle for her? Her conflicted feelings for Peeta, the boy who once showed her kindness.

They are both aboard the tribute train, and meet Haymitch for the first time. Haymitch is a drunk, and proceeds to vomit. Peeta offers to help him to his room and get him cleaned up.

Why would he do that? Katniss wonders. To curry favor with their mentor? Or because he is fundamentally a kind person? Just like when he gave her bread? This kicks Katniss in the heart:

The idea pulls me up short. A kind Peeta Mellark is far more dangerous to me than an unkind one. Kind people have a way of working their way inside me and rooting there. And I can't let Peeta do this. Not where we're going. So I decide, from this moment on, to have as little as possible to do with the baker's son.

These conflicting feelings persist throughout the chapter, which ends:

All the pieces are still fitting together, but I sense he has a plan forming. He hasn't accepted his death. He is already fighting hard to stay alive. Which also means that kind Peeta Mellark, the boy who gave me the bread, is fighting hard to kill me.

In *To Kill a Mockingbird*, Scout is thrust through The Doorway of No Return #1 by virtue of the fact that her father, Atticus, undertakes the defense of a black man, Tom Robinson, on charges he raped a white girl. In the south of that era, an impossible job.

Scout gets a Kick in the Shins soon after when she and her brother Jem encounter the old widow Mrs. Henry Lafayette Dubose.

Mrs. Dubose represents the old south and its view of the races. This is going to be the central struggle within Scout. Will she grow up and become another Mrs. Dubose? (This would be psychological death.) Or will she learn to see all people as worthy of equal dignity?

Mrs. Dubose starts giving the two children a scolding for not being in school. Jem explains it's Saturday.

But Mrs. Dubose is not going to let facts stand in her way. She's mad, as she always is about something.

She turns her "arthritic finger" on Scout and castigates her for wearing overalls. Such a girl is liable to end up waiting on tables at the O.K. Café! Mrs. Dubose continues:

"Not only a Finch waiting on tables but one in the courthouse lawing for niggers!"

Jem stiffened. Mrs. Dubose's shot had gone home and she knew it.

"Yes indeed, what has this world come to when a Finch goes against his raising? I'll tell you!" She put her hand to her mouth. When she drew it away, it trailed a long silver thread of saliva. "Your father's no better than the niggers and trash he works for!"

Later in the chapter, Atticus warns Scout:

"[W]hen summer comes you'll have to keep your head about far worse things ... It's not fair for you and Jem. I know that, but sometimes we have to make the best of things, and the way we conduct ourselves when the chips are down—well, all I can say is, when you and Jem are grown, maybe you'll look back on this with some compassion and some feeling that I didn't let you down."

See how this first big obstacle is one that is connected to the whole story? It's mainly an interior moment.

In an action novel, the kick is usually an outer obstacle. *Lethal Weapon* provides an example.

After Riggs and Murtaugh are partnered up (Doorway #1, forcing them to pursue a case together, one that is about a whole lot more than they realize), they go to interview a witness about the victim's death. What does said witness do? Talk? No, starts a gunfight! Murtaugh shoots him in the leg, but Riggs shoots to kill.

This is amped-up trouble. Why did this have to happen? They will soon find out, but not yet. With a Kick in the Shins, the bigger story question remains a bit of a mystery.

Why This Works

A Kick in the Shins is part of the building process. Trouble needs to mount as the novel progresses. This beat is the first hit of Act II. It is crucial for the readers to experience. It instills in them confidence that the rest of the book is going to have more and bigger obstacles for the Lead.

Helpful Hints for Plotters and Pantsers

Both plotters and pantsers can brainstorm scenes at any time. So try this: come up with a long list of obstacles and opposition characters that can be thrown in the Lead's way. Go crazy. When you've got fifteen or twenty of these, choose the best ones and list them in order from bad to worse to worst.

The one that's bad is the Kick in the Shins.

Super Structure Reminder

Remember: Trouble is your business! Don't be hesitant about plying your trade in every scene of your book.

7

The Mirror Moment

This beat is so important I wrote a whole book about it called *Write Your Novel From the Middle.* I will give you the gist of it here as one of the signposts.

I discovered what I call the "mirror moment" by studying the so-called midpoint. In looking at the books and blogs on fiction craft, I did not find uniformity of agreement on what the midpoint is supposed to do.

Some definitions were fine and workable, but not all that compelling to me. Others were too academic or theoretical.

I wondered if there really was anything unique about the midpoint. Couldn't it just be another in a series of rising-action scenes in Act II? Why did it have to be something special?

So I decided to check it out for myself.

I took a few of my favorite movies and used the timer to go to the exact middle of the films. The movies were *Casablanca, The Fugitive, Lethal Weapon,* and *Moonstruck.*

What I found absolutely floored me.

Then I took a couple of favorite novels, *The Hunger Games* and *Gone with the Wind,* and opened up to the physical middles and rooted around.

And I found the same thing.

Which floored me again.

What I found was a moment where the main character has to figuratively look at himself, as in the mirror. He is confronted with a disturbing truth: change or die.

Let's take *Casablanca*. Rick has come to Casablanca to forget Ilsa Lund, the woman who (he thinks) betrayed him. But then Ilsa comes walking into his café one night, with her husband, Victor Laszlo!

This is the Doorway of No Return #1, by the way. It forces the confrontations in the rest of the movie.

Rick handles this development like a hearty American male of the 1940s—he gets drunk. He sits in his saloon after hours with Sam, the piano player, and drinks and has a flashback about Paris. That's where he met Ilsa. They fell in love. Rick proposes marriage. But when the train was pulling out of the station for the last time, Ilsa was not there.

After the flashback, we are back in the saloon with a toasted Rick. Then Ilsa walks in. She has come to explain why she left him in Paris. She'd found out that her husband, whom she thought had died in a concentration camp, was alive. She pleads with Rick to understand. But Rick is so bitter he essentially calls her a whore:

"Tell me, who was it you left me for? Was it Laszlo, or were there others in between? Or aren't you the kind that tells?"

Tears coursing down her cheek, Ilsa sees that this is not the same man she once loved. She leaves without another word.

Rick, full of self-disgust, puts his head in his hands. He is thinking along the lines of, "What kind of man am I to do something like that?"

He is looking in the mirror. At himself.

The rest of the film will determine whether he stays a selfish drunk or regains his humanity. And that is what Casablanca is truly about, in both narrative and theme.

It's about psychological life and death.

There's one other kind of mirror moment, usually found in

an action film. It's when the character looks at her situation and thinks, "The odds are too great. I can't possibly survive. I'm probably going to die."

Such a moment is right in the middle of *The Hunger Games.* Here is the paragraph:

> I know the end is coming. My legs are shaking and my heart is too quick . . . My fingers stroke the smooth ground, sliding easily across the top. *This is an okay place to die,* I think.

There is also a moment like this in *The Fugitive.* In the middle of the film Dr. Richard Kimble is living in a rented basement. Suddenly, cops are all over the place, guns drawn, surrounding it! Kimble is trapped like a rat.

Only it turns out the cops have come for the landlady's son, a suspected drug dealer.

Kimble, realizing this, his nerves shot, breaks down.

In a novel, you might write his inner thoughts. *I can't do this anymore. Who am I kidding? I'm not a street criminal. The whole U.S. Department of Justice is after me, not to mention the Chicago Police. I'm not going to make it!*

So, two kinds of mirror moments:

1. Who am I? What have I become? What do I have to do to change?
2. I can't possibly win this battle. I'm going to die.

The first type of mirror moment tells the character he has to grow into a different and better person (if he doesn't, we have a tragedy).

The second type requires that the character grow stronger, in order to survive.

Your mirror moment will turn on the lights. It will illumine everything else in your novel.

The mirror moment works in any kind of novel. For

example, if the book is about a woman trying to break free from a dominating mother, the mirror moment could be the "I'm probably going to die" type. In this case, die psychologically.

That is the mirror moment in the classic Bette Davis film *Now, Voyager*. Davis plays Charlotte Vale, a "homely" woman of no special talent who has been psychologically damaged by her family, especially her strong-willed mother. When at last Charlotte breaks free and begins to find her true self (with the help of a man who falls in love with her), she has to come back home and face her mother again.

There is a tense battle right in the middle of the movie. And Charlotte begins to think she will have to go back to being her old self. She is facing psychological death.

Which way will she go? Will she become stronger? (It's a Bette Davis movie, so you can probably guess the answer!)

On the other hand, even the genre-iest of genre book benefits from a mirror moment.

Case in point: *The Executioner* series begun by Don Pendleton. These are stripped-down, full-throttle male action adventure novels. Average body count? Double digits per book. Virtually all of them tallied by the lead character, one Mack "The Executioner" Bolan.

How have these books done? Well, there are now over 600 titles in the series, as well as spin-offs (other authors have done the duties after Pendleton's run was over). Hundreds of millions sold.

I always like to read the first book in a series, so I got my hands on #1, *War Against the Mafia* (1969).

Mack Bolan is not the introspective type. He is an ex-Green Beret sniper who served in Vietnam where he had at least ninety-seven kills.

During his service his father got on the bad side of the Mafia. The result: his father, mother and sister are all dead.

For that, Bolan is going to make the whole Mafia pay.

The back cover of the book describes Bolan this way: *He's hard-hitting, ruthless, and without a trace of sentimentality.*

You might not expect a mirror moment of any kind in such a book. But here it is, right in the middle:

> Everybody would be after him now—the cops, the Mafia, the contract killers, probably the whole damn world. Bolan shivered slightly.
>
> Fear is a natural emotion, he told himself. *Use it! Make it work for you!* It was a pep talk he had used many times before. But then, he had never been completely alone before ... How long could he evade them? Not long, he was realist enough to understand that fact. He had, probably, a few days at the most. A few days. Well—he'd have to do what he had to do in a few days. He had to crack the Mafia wide open, get them running scared, evade their killers, evade the cops, and keep himself from coming unglued in the process—all in a matter of two or three days. Could he do it? He patted the big Marlin. Well—he'd do it or die. It was that simple.

Why This Works

In my humble opinion, the mirror moment is the most potent of all the signposts. It takes you to the heart of your story. It helps you determine exactly the kind of novel you want to write—or that your writer mind is trying to *tell* you to write.

It's like a search light on the top of a hill helping you see both directions on the highway.

Helpful Hints for Plotters and Pantsers

Outliners: How do you direct your mind to come up with scene ideas? You can of course use the signpost prompts, but your ideas will be subject to change as you learn more about your plot. Why not learn the most important thing first? Brainstorm the mirror moment up front. Then when you conceive and outline scenes they will have an organic unity to them.

And pantsers, you love to start down the novel road with nary a care, don't you? You have your bindle on your shoulder and whistle a happy tune. You don't know where you're going but you're sure you'll end up somewhere. Only "somewhere" can turn out to be a dark cave with thick walls. You have to back out and retrace your steps and try another direction — which can lead to another cave.

So have your fun and write, but stop about five thousand or ten thousand words in and smell the roses. And as you do, brainstorm a possible mirror moment. Write the scene. Feel it. You're a pantser, after all. You can write out of order with no problem. Only this time you'll write something that clarifies and sends you out in the right direction.

Super Structure Reminder

The biggest changes we make in our own lives occur when we are thrust into a crisis. Enduring fiction is built upon that same thing: it's about how a character, through force of will, fights life-threatening challenges and is transformed because of it. It's only when we feel we *must* change that we *do* change. The mirror moment makes that clear to the character and, most important of all, to the reader.

8

Pet the Dog

Let's imagine that Dirty Harry Callahan is in a shootout, at night, on a dark San Francisco street (not too hard to do that, is it?). He's got his .44 Magnum at the ready. He's leaning on the wall in an alley. A bullet bursts a brick next to his head.

Trouble. More shots are sure to be fired in his direction.

Clank!

Behind him!

Harry whirls around, aiming his gun.

Only it's just a garbage can that's been overturned. And out from behind comes a scraggly little dog.

The dog walks over to Dirty Harry, wagging his tail.

Harry looks down, annoyed. "You better get outta here, fella."

The dog goes nowhere.

Harry leans over and picks up the dog with one arm.

"Didn't you hear me?"

The dog licks Harry's face.

Harry issues a low growl.

Dog licks his face again.

Another shot!

Harry runs with the dog down the alley, out of harm's way. The shooter gets away. But the dog is safe.

What Harry did was stop in the middle of his own troubles to help out something weaker than himself.

This is the Pet-the-Dog beat.

Coming sometime within Act II (usually just before or just after the mirror moment scene), the Pet-the-Dog beat shows that the Lead has heart. Maybe it's a reluctant heart, but he follows it nonetheless.

And it bonds the reader even tighter to the main character.

You'll find Pet-the-Dog beats all over classic books and movies.

Have you ever seen the romantic comedy *It Happened One Night?* No? Go watch it now. I'll wait.

Welcome back. *It Happened One Night* was the biggest hit of 1934 and shot Clark Gable into superstardom. It swept the Academy Awards.

It's the story of spoiled heiress Ellie Andrews (Claudette Colbert) who wants to marry a rich guy her father thinks is a big phony. She is being held captive on her father's yacht and escapes by jumping overboard and swimming away.

Now alone (for the first time in her life) she's trying to get to New York to meet up with her lover.

But she has no street smarts and her picture is plastered all over the newspapers.

Enter Peter Warne (Clark Gable), a down-on-his-luck journalist who sees the scoop of the century. He offers to help Ellie get to New York if she'll give him her story exclusive.

So begins the road trip.

They start off traveling by night bus. With only a few bucks between them, Peter tells Ellie they are on a strict budget. Things seem to be working out until the bus runs into a ditch. The people in the bus fall all over themselves. Peter and Ellie are laughing about it, until they hear the anguished cry of a little boy.

"Ma! Ma!"

He's over his mother who has passed out.

Peter goes to help. He orders Ellie to get some water. She brings it. Peter gives the woman a drink and she starts to come around.

Peter and Ellie try to console the boy. He says he and his Ma haven't eaten since the day before. His mother spent all their money for the bus tickets so they could get to New York where there is the possibility of a job for her.

"Going without food is bad business, son," Peter says. "Why didn't you ask somebody?

"I was gonna do it, but Ma wouldn't let me. She was ashamed, I guess."

Peter reaches in his pocket and takes out the only bill he has. As he's checking for more Ellie snatches it and gives it to the boy. The boy protests he shouldn't take it. "You might need it," he says.

They do, of course. But Peter says, "Forget it, son. I got millions."

That's a Pet-the-Dog moment, giving us greater sympathy for Peter Warne, and a touch more for Ellie, the spoiled heiress (for whom money is a non-issue).

The Fugitive has a brilliant Pet-the-Dog scene in Act II. Richard Kimble is posing as a hospital janitor so he can access the prosthetics records and close in on the one-armed man. As he's slipping out of the hospital he finds himself waylaid by traffic on the trauma floor.

As he waits for a chance to move he notices a little boy on a gurney, groaning. From the look on Kimble's face we know he wants to help that boy, but can't without giving himself away. A doctor gives a cursory look at the chest x-ray, calls out that the kid is okay.

The supervising doctor sees Kimble and asks him to wheel the kid down to an observation room. So off Kimble goes with the gurney.

As he does, he asks the boy where it hurts. He slips the x-ray from its envelope and holds it up to the light.

He determines that the boy needs immediate surgery. So on the elevator he changes the boy's orders and takes him to an operating room, turning him over to a surgeon who gets the boy in for the help he needs.

So Kimble saves a boy's life at the risk of being found out. And the filmmakers use it for just that purpose. The doctor on the trauma floor saw Kimble looking at the film. She catches up to him and confronts him. Not satisfied with his evasions, she grabs his ID badge and calls for Security.

Kimble's Pet-the-Dog moment has gotten him into worse trouble.

Note that. Pet-the-Dog is best when it threatens and even exposes the Lead to danger.

Can you name the Pet-the-Dog sequence in *The Hunger Games?* Of course you can. Just ask yourself when it is that Katniss helps somebody weaker, risking her own neck in the process.

It's when she helps Rue, of course.

You can see the relationship between Pet-the-Dog and the Care Package. The difference is that the Care Package is about an existing relationship before the story begins. Pet-the-Dog is a sudden, new relationship that springs up in the midst of the trouble of Act II.

Why This Works

As was seen with the Care Package, we are sympathetically drawn to characters who don't only think of themselves. A Pet-the-Dog moment intensifies that feeling for the reader.

Helpful Hints for Plotters and Pantsers

You plotters can come up with a Pet-the-Dog scene and use it to develop a new character (such as Rue). You can move that scene around as your outline grows, giving it a strategic location. For example, if you have a scene of particular intensity and leave off on a cliffhanger, a Pet-the-Dog beat can stretch out the tension while, at the same time, illustrating the humanity of your hero.

Pantsers, one of your challenges is coming to your writing day having no idea what to write next. One of the techniques to help you out of this is to introduce a new character. If you're well into your story, try using Pet-the-Dog to do that. Give us a new character that your Lead must help in some way.

Super Structure Reminder

If the Lead thinks only of himself the readers get a negative impression, subtle as that may be. Petting the dog adds a much-needed counter to that vibe. It can be as big as saving a life, or as small as giving a kind word to someone in need.

9

Doorway of No Return #2

Doorway of No Return #2 is so designated because, once again, there is no going back. The Lead passes through the door that makes inevitable the final battle and resolution.

Let's begin our discussion with what happens in Act II. This is where the major action takes place. The stakes are death (physical, professional or psychological) and the Lead has to fight.

The second act is a series of scenes where the character confronts and resists death, and is opposed by counter forces.

In Act II of *Gone with the Wind*, Scarlett has to get out of Atlanta with Melanie and her baby before the Yankees arrive.

She needs to get money to save Tara from onerous taxes.

She needs to figure out how to handle that charmer, Rhett Butler, who keeps showing up in her life.

And so on.

Then Scarlett passes through Doorway #2 and finds herself in Act III.

In a novel, the second doorway is a major crisis or setback, or some sort of clue or discovery. One of these sends the action toward the Final Battle.

In *GWTW*, the second doorway is a major setback. Scarlett's husband, Frank Kennedy, is shot dead. That leaves Scarlett a widow, until she consents to marry Rhett.

This marriage is going to make inevitable the final battle in Scarlett's heart. She still believes *she belonged to Ashley, forever and ever.* The crisis intensifies. Rhett finally realizes Scarlett will never give up on Ashley, and decides to leave the marriage. Scarlett, however, has a final realization of her own: she has been living for a false dream. Home and Rhett are what she truly needs. But it comes too late. Rhett doesn't give a damn, and Scarlett will have to return to Tara to think about getting him back. Tomorrow.

Here are other examples of this Doorway of No Return #2:

- Hannibal Lecter tells Clarice Starling that Buffalo Bill covets what he sees every day. Clue! This information leads Clarice to the killer. *(The Silence of the Lambs)*
- The bullet-ridden body of a bundle-carrying ship's captain collapses in Sam Spade's office. Inside the bundle is the black bird. Major discovery! *(The Maltese Falcon)*
- Tom Robinson, an innocent black man, is found guilty of rape by an all-white jury, despite the evidence. Major set-back! *(To Kill a Mockingbird)*

Why This Works

Unless there is a way to get to the final battle, Act II will go on forever. The natural rhythm of the three-act structure dictates that this second doorway open up with about one quarter or a little less of the book left.

Helpful Hints for Plotters and Pantsers

Plotters, this second doorway is often best left unspecified until you are well into your novel or outlining. The content of the scene will be affected by all that you have decided up to this point. Characters you have fleshed out, scenes that you have written with happy surprises, new events that you've added to the book as you've written along—all of these will give you possibilities for the Doorway of No Return #2.

Pantsers, you love the idea of discovery, so this is one signpost you can look to with eager anticipation. I suggest you just think about it from time to time. Get your writer's mind chugging away on it while you do your daily, happy writing. You'll probably find yourself thinking of several possibilities well before you get to that scene. Write those ideas down. One of them may very well be the one you need.

Super Structure Reminder

Readers do not like to see the Lead helped out of trouble via coincidence. So don't let this second doorway seem to offer that. A crisis or setback can happen that way, because it's not help. It's more trouble. But a discovery or clue ought to happen because the Lead has done something to find it, or earn it. It's the result of her efforts or cogitation that opens the door.

10

Mounting Forces

We are through the second Doorway of No Return. Soon the Final Battle must be fought. There's no going back to Kansas unless this last challenge is met.

The opposition, knowing the Final Battle is closing in fast, gathers his forces.

In *Gone With the Wind,* Scarlett has lost her husband, Frank. But she marries Rhett, and we are in Act III. She bears Rhett a daughter, Bonnie Blue Butler.

But she is still in love with Ashley, and Rhett knows it.

It's a power struggle between them, over how they will conduct themselves—Scarlett does not want any more children; Rhett wants respectability for his daughter. Scarlett wants to sleep alone. Rhett consorts with Belle Watling, the madam of a bordello.

Then one night Rhett plays his strongest hand—physically. He carries Scarlett up to their room and forces himself on her.

How will Scarlett deal with that? The rest of Act III tells the story.

In *Lethal Weapon* Murtaugh confronts his war buddy in his house in Malibu. He knows the death of the guy's daughter is tied to drug trafficking. Ex-CIA mercs are running it. Murtaugh says he'll bring it down, but his buddy says, "It's too big." Murtaugh insists he's not going to leave without getting the whole story.

But then! A helicopter rises up out of nowhere. Sitting in the helicopter is Gary Busey with a rifle.

Gary Busey with any sort of weapon is never a good thing, no matter what movie you're watching.

To prove this point, Busey shoots Murtaugh's buddy.

The forces have mounted in a big way. The mercs know what's up, are willing to murder people over it, and now it is going to be a battle to the death.

In *To Kill a Mockingbird,* some time after Tom Robinson is convicted (major setback), Tom Ewell seeks out Atticus Finch and spits on him, daring him to fight. Atticus does not, but clearly Jem and Scout see the danger. They think Atticus ought to start packing a gun.

There is a double barrel to the forces in the book. Physical danger toward Atticus from Ewell, and psychological danger for Scout from the ladies in town. They want to make sure Scout grows up to be like them. When the missionary society meets at the Finch household, Scout must wear a dress. The dress is a symbol of Southern ladyhood. But Scout is not absorbed yet. She is wearing her britches under the dress!

The ladies all call her "Jean Louise ," her proper name. Scout tells us this was all a part of Aunt Alexandra's "campaign to teach me to be a lady." The forces of Southern ways are mounting to mold Scout Finch!

Why This Works

Mounting Forces is perhaps the most logical beat in all of Super Structure. By Act III, the momentum toward the end is relentless. Remember Wells Root's picture of the rushing river? Act III is like going over a waterfall. You can't stop it. The antagonist knows this, and gathers his strength. He knows what kind of death is on the line, so it's logical that he makes preparations for the Final Battle.

Helpful Hints for Plotters and Pantsers

Back in the discussion on the Kick in the Shins, I suggested that you make a long list of possible obstacles and put them in order from bad to worse to worst. Mounting Forces should be a "worse" beat. The worst is yet to come, when the lights go out (that's our next section).

So go back to your list, or create some new possibilities. Brainstorming lists is one of the most best creative exercises for the fiction writer. Plotters and pantsers both can do this at any time in the writing process.

Super Structure Reminder

No matter what kind of novel you write, the story ought to feel like the trash compactor in *Star Wars*. Your Lead is thrust into the situation of the novel. Then notices the walls starting to close in. In Act II, he's still got time to get out of danger. But in Act III time has run out. The walls are about to crush him.

11

Lights Out

The deepest darkness.

The blackest night.

The point when all seems lost.

This is Lights Out. This is where it looks as if the Lead can't possibly win in his struggle with death.

It may be that the forces arrayed against him are too strong.

Or it may be a dilemma that leaves no good choice.

This is where you have the readers biting their figurative nails. Or even real nails.

You want them thinking, "There's no way out!"

It's what the Lead is thinking, too.

Here are a few examples.

In *Lethal Weapon*, Riggs has been captured by the bad guys. The very bad guys. Guys so bad they hire Gary Busey to do their dirty work.

That work in this instance is dangling Riggs by his arms under a water pipe that is drenching him. The reason? A man is about to inflict major electrical pain on Riggs by way of jumper cables and a car battery. The torture is to get Riggs to talk about a shipment of heroin.

And Gary Busey is standing there to watch.

There is no way Martin Riggs is going to survive this.

Or is there?

Lights out usually happens close to the final battle, so the ending of the book feels like a runaway train.

In *Gone with the Wind*, Scarlett is heading toward a crisis with Rhett and Ashley and Melanie and her whole life. She's holding on to her dreams by a hair.

And then the world goes dark.

Her daughter with Rhett, Bonnie Blue Butler, is killed when she falls from a pony.

After that, the events of the book cascade like water off a cliff.

In *The Hunger Games*, things go from bad to worse very quickly as we head toward the end. Katniss and Peeta have made it to the Cornucopia, along with Cato, but they are all being chased by the muttations!

Cato gets Peeta in a headlock as Katniss readies an arrow. Cato laughs. "Shoot me and he goes down with me."

This is Lights Out because of the terrible dilemma, as Katniss explains:

He's right. If I take him out and he falls to the mutts, Peeta is sure to die with him. We've reached a stalemate. I can't shoot Cato without killing Peeta, too. He can't kill Peeta without guaranteeing an arrow in his brain. We stand like statues, both of us seeking an out.

In *To Kill a Mockingbird*, the narrator, Scout (as an adult) tells us when the lights are about to go out. It's at the end of Chapter 27: *Jem said he would take me. Thus began our longest journey together.*

It's not a long journey by physical distance. It's a journey into the deepest fears of childhood. Would they emerge whole?

It's the night of the Halloween pageant, and Scout went dressed as a giant ham.

This is, of course, when Bob Ewell attacks them in the dark.

When Jem is injured and Scout knocked to the ground in her ham costume.

Like most great literary fiction, *To Kill a Mockingbird* is about inner transformation. Scout will move from innocence to awareness, from childishness to budding maturity.

How will she handle what has happened to her and Jem? That's the question we ask when the lights go out.

Why This Works

My friend and teaching colleague, Christopher Vogler (author of *The Writer's Journey: Mythic Structure for Writers),* calls this a "death-and-rebirth" beat. The hero must "shed the personality of the journey and build a new one that is suitable for return to the Ordinary World." There is a final "cleansing" that takes place.

What this accomplishes in the audience, says Vogler, is a *catharsis.* In a satisfying story, the audience moves beyond mere narrative to an actual "expansion of awareness."

This is always most effectively realized when the lights go out.

Now what? That is the subject of the next chapter.

Helpful Hints for Plotters and Pantsers

Whether you plot or pants your way through a draft, you should constantly be listening to your writer's mind and tweak it to come up with possible endings. What you want is a list of several.

Plotters can do this at the beginning.

Pantsers can do this during, keeping track of the ideas as they occur.

One of those will be your actual ending.

But don't discard the list. Use one of the remaining choices as a Lights Out beat!

Nothing is wasted in this thing called writing.

Super Structure Reminder

Some of the greatest endings—like *Casablanca*—involve sacrifice. Rebirth can only follow death, and death is very often the sacrifice of the thing the Lead wants most. It may be his very life, as in *Spartacus* and *Braveheart*.

12

Q Factor

The Q Factor is named for the character in the James Bond movies, the old fellow at headquarters who gives Bond his gadgets and tells him not to play with them. There is a very important reason this character exists.

Let's cut ahead to the inevitable James Bond ending. Bond is hanging by his ankles over a school of piranha. The bad guy grins and says something like, "Enjoy your swim, Mr. Bond." Then he sets the timer to lower James Bond into the pool of man-eating fish and, of course, leaves. (An interesting existential puzzle is why villains so often leave before their adversaries are dispatched.)

As Bond is lowered toward his doom, he manages to get his thumb on one of his cufflinks. The cufflink turns into a small, rotating saw. He uses that saw to cut through the restraints on his hands.

Now he is able to reach into his jacket pocket and pull out a fountain pen. The fountain pen is, in reality, a device that holds a compressed nitrogen charge and shoots a small grappling hook and line across the piranha pond, enabling Bond to swing to safety on the other side of the pool.

Now, if we had been reading along in the story and Bond

simply produced those items for the first time, we'd all be groaning. How convenient! What a cheat!

But of course, it was all set up by the Q scene. Because we saw these items before, we accept them when they come out at the right time.

In fiction, the Lead character reaches a point near the end when everything looks lost.

Lights Out.

What he needs is courage and motivation for the Final Battle. This is where the Q Factor comes in.

Q is an emotional impetus that is set up in Act I that that comes back to provide inspiration or instruction at a critical moment in Act III.

Sometimes the Q Factor is an icon of some sort, a physical object, like the mockingjay pin Katniss touches just before the Final Battle in *The Hunger Games.*

Sometimes it is the memory of a beloved mentor. Luke Skywalker hears Obi-Wan reminding him to "use the Force." In the old Warner Bros. movies of the 30s, you would often have a scene where the Lead, facing the Final Battle, hears the voice of his mother, or a priest, or his girl, telling him he can do it! He can fight and win!

Simply put, something happens that draws courage from the moral and emotional reservoir of the Lead.

In the great Frank Capra movie *Mr. Smith Goes to Washington,* the naïve young senator played by James Stewart arrives in Washington D.C. for the first time. He is mesmerized by the city that represents everything he loves about America. So he slips away from his handlers and goes on a sightseeing tour, rendered in a wonderful montage. The montage ends at the Lincoln Memorial. Here, young Jefferson Smith is deeply moved. He reads the words of the Gettysburg Address inscribed on the wall. He sees a young boy holding his grandfather's hand, trying to read those words aloud.

He observes an African-American gentleman removing his hat in respect.

Smith looks back up at the face of Lincoln.

We now have this emotional moment embedded in our minds.

Near the end, Mr. Smith realizes he's been a stooge, used as a puppet by a corrupt political machine. He has even been betrayed by the senior senator who had been a good friend of his own father. Smith takes this as the final knife in his back and decides to leave town.

It's nighttime, and he is passing the Lincoln Memorial, but this time defeated and downcast. He sits heavily on the steps.

Along comes the political operative played by Jean Arthur. Originally she thought of Smith as a dumb oaf too, but she has come to respect his integrity in this sea of cynicism. She says, "I thought I'd find you here." And then she tells him, "Remember the day you got here? Remember what you said about Mr. Lincoln? You said he was sitting up there waiting for someone to come along. You were right. He was waiting for man who could see his job and sail into it, that's what he was waiting for. A man who could tear into the Taylors and root 'em out into the open. I think he was waiting for you, Jeff. He knows you can do that, and so do I."

Abraham Lincoln is Jefferson Smith's Q Factor. All the emotion he felt in that first visit to the monument wells up in him. He's ready for the Final Battle, as impossible as it may seem.

Sometimes, the Q Factor can be a negative emotion. In *High Noon*, the classic western starring Gary Cooper as Will Kane, Kane finds himself about to face four killers, alone. The towns-people have all come up with excuses not to help him. He knows he will probably die. And the real bummer is that he has just married Grace Kelly!

There comes a point just before the climax when Kane is considering getting on a horse and riding out of town. He will get together with his wife again and go off somewhere and open a store.

Of course, if he does this, he will die psychologically. He will be a coward. He will have failed in his sworn duty as a lawman, too.

So he's having to choose between physical death and psychological death.

Bummer.

Enter the character of Harvey, played by Lloyd Bridges. Harvey is a true coward, and has chafed under the shadow of the great Will Kane. He sees Kane and knows that if he can get him to ride out of town, in effect showing the town that Kane is really a coward after all, then he, Harvey, will look good in comparison.

As Harvey tries to get Kane to do this, Kane realizes that if he does go, he will in fact be no better than Harvey. And that's when he makes the decision to stay. Harvey, who was introduced early in the film, is the negative Q Factor for Kane's decision.

Why This Works

Great stories are about death, and when facing death a character must deal with *fear*. Fear manifests itself most when all the forces are marshaled against the Lead. Fear and common sense tell the Lead to give up, run away.

What makes him stay and fight? The Q Factor, an emotional element that comes in when needed most.

Helpful Hints for Plotters and Pantsers

Brainstorm possible Q Factors. Include physical items, mentors, and characters who could embody cowardice or moral compromise. Choose the one you like best as a Q Factor.

Next, write a scene early in Act I that anchors this element *emotionally* to the Lead. Like Smith looking at the face of Lincoln, or Will Kane being repulsed by Harvey.

It's also helpful to refer to the Q Factor once in Act II, as a reminder. You should do this subtly, almost as a throwaway. Just enough so the reader has it in mind when it finally pays off.

The Q Factor is mobile. It can be placed before or after Lights Out in Act III. Put it where it feels right.

Super Structure Reminder

A novel is about a character using *strength of will* to fight the forces of death. This fight cannot just be analytical. We are moved to action through emotion, not simply logic.

13

Final Battle

Every great ending is a Final Battle inside or outside the main character. Sometimes a mixture of both.

By outside, I mean the physical force arrayed against the Lead. This can be as big as the armies of an empire—as in *Star Wars*—or as intimate as the physical stammer suffered by Prince Albert in *The King's Speech*.

The question is: will the Lead muster the courage to fight? Will he overcome?

By inside the character, I mean a psychological battle that has to be resolved. Will the Lead show the courage that allows him to be transformed?

In *Casablanca*, for example, the Final Battle is inside Rick (Humphrey Bogart). He has spent the whole movie as the anti-hero, not taking a stand against the Nazis. Then the love of his life, Ilsa (Ingrid Bergman) comes to his saloon, with her husband, the war hero Victor Laszlo (Paul Henreid). At the end, Rick can have Ilsa back. She has consented to leave with Rick.

And, come on, it's *Ingrid Bergman!* Talk about having your ideal within reach!

But if he does take her, he'll be violating a central moral

tenet of society. The writers also set up that it will devastate Laszlo, thus hurting the war effort itself.

Rick has to make an inner battle decision, and ultimately sacrifices what he wants most in the world for a greater good. It becomes the most famous ending in Hollywood history when he gets an unexpected reward—the French police captain, Louis (Claude Rains) does not arrest Rick for murdering the Nazi major. Instead, they go off together to rejoin the war effort. It's "the beginning of a beautiful friendship."

In *Star Wars*, the Final Battle is an actual battle. Luke must find the will and way to fly his X-wing into the Death Star.

In *The Hunger Games*, which is filled with physical battles, the Final Battle comes down to another dilemma for Katniss. After rescuing Peeta from Cato's grip, there is a stunning announcement from Claudius Templesmith. The recently changed rule allowing *two* winners has been reversed! Now there will be only one!

Katniss and Peeta are the only two contestants left.

Who is going to kill whom?

How will Katniss solve this final battle of wills with the Gamemakers?

She solves it with a brilliant move. Knowing the Capitol needs a victor in the games, she and Peeta agree to poison themselves. Just as they are about to do it, the rule change is reversed again! Both Katniss and Peeta are declared the winners.

In *Lethal Weapon*, we have a huge physical battle at the end, where Riggs and Murtaugh take on the traffickers to the death. It comes down to a physical fight between Riggs and Mr. Joshua (Gary Busey). Riggs bests him but decides to let the cops arrest him.

But Riggs has to learn a hard lesson: never turn your back on Gary Busey. Mr. Joshua grabs a cop's gun and is about to fire, but Riggs and Murtaugh both draw theirs and blow Mr. Joshua away.

Why This Works

The Final Battle is the whole point of the novel. It's what every-thing is leading up to. Without it, there is no resolution, no satis-faction, no coming away from the story with a feeling of completeness. The Final Battle works simply because *it has to be there or there is no story at all.*

Helpful Hints for Plotters and Pantsers

How do you create the perfect Final Battle for your hero? Look to the Mirror Moment!

If your hero has had one of those "I'm probably going to die" moments, then your Final Battle will most likely be physical.

If it's a "Who am I/What have I become?" moment, then the Final Battle will likely be an interior battle, a dilemma.

Super Structure Reminder

One way to describe the arc of a satisfying story is that it is, in the end, a quest for *courage*. In an outside-forces-type of ending, as in a thriller, the Lead must find the courage to fight against overwhelming odds. If he dies, we have one kind of tragedy, as in *Hamlet*. If it's inside, the Lead must find the moral courage to do the right thing. If he doesn't, the story becomes another kind of tragedy, the Lead left to suffer the consequences, as in *Hud*, the Paul Newman movie (based on *Horseman, Pass By* by Larry McMurtry).

14

Transformation

The last beat in Super Structure is the Transformation. It's the coda, the resonance, the final note. Done skillfully it will leave readers so wonderfully satisfied they will seek out your other books with enthusiasm and discretionary income.

Which is what you want.

But if the final note is flat, the enthusiasm won't be there.

So what is the source of that wonderful feeling at the end?

In short, it is Transformation.

The character has changed in a significant way.

Either by becoming essentially a new person, or by becoming stronger.

Rick Blaine in *Casablanca* is a new person at the end.

Dr. Richard Kimble in *The Fugitive* is still the same, decent person he always was—but he is much stronger in terms of courage and inner strength because he had to fight against such terrible odds.

Notice how these two types of transformation are tied to the Mirror Moment.

If the character looks at himself, thinking *Who am I?*, it means he has to become a different person.

If he looks at himself and thinks, *I'm probably going to die*, it means he has to get stronger in order to live.

The events of the story, remember, are about fighting off death. No one comes out of that the same.

Your final pages need to prove the transformation.

If your character, like Richard Kimble, has become stronger, just the fact of survival and return to normalcy is often enough. At the end of *The Fugitive*, Kimble is in the back of a car with Sam Gerard, the lawman who has been chasing him this whole time.

"I thought you didn't care," Kimble says.

"I don't," says Gerard, then laughs. "Don't tell anybody, okay?"

And off they go, delivering Kimble back to his own world.

There's a similar beat in *Fargo*. Marge Gunderson remains the same, good, decent police woman she's always been. But she's just caught a horrific murderer at the wood chipper.

Driving back with this monster in the back of her patrol car, she says to him, "So that was Mrs. Lundegaard on the floor in there. And I guess that was your accomplice in the wood chipper. And those three people in Brainerd. And for what? For a little bit of money. There's more to life than a little money, you know. Don't you know that? And here you are, and it's a beautiful day. Well. I just don't understand it."

Marge is the stronger now. She got the killer. But she's the same person.

In a case where the character changes fundamentally, it is best to prove the transformation by *showing* it.

In *Casablanca*, Rick has learned that there is something bigger to live for than the problems of "three small people." There is a larger context, a universal concern for the community.

To prove that, he not only tells Ilsa to get on the plane with Laszlo, he makes sure it happens by holding a gun on Louis, the

French police captain, and then actually shooting the Nazi major, Strasser, as he tries to stop the plane.

Talk about proof! Rick has sacrificed his very life for the principle he has come to believe.

My favorite proof of transformation comes from *Lethal Weapon*. Riggs starts out as a suicidal loner. He ends up coming back to life through the loyalty of his partner, Murtaugh, and the warmth of Murtaugh's family.

Back in the Argument Against Transformation, Riggs had shown Murtaugh the hollow-point bullet he was saving to blow his head off someday.

Now here at the end, Riggs shows up at Murtaugh's house on Christmas Eve, and Murtaugh's daughter answers the doorbell. Riggs says he has a present for her to give to her dad.

He pulls out the bullet with a little bow around it. "Tell him I won't be needing it anymore."

Transformation proved.

Why This Works

A story isn't over until the character changes.

Or, in some cases, refuses to change—which makes for tragedy.

On rare occasions, the change (or not) may be left hanging in the air. Ambiguous endings are usually the stuff of literary novels, such as *The Catcher in the Rye*. It's up to the reader to decide if Holden Caulfield will ever get out of that sanitarium healed.

In all other cases, show us the transformation.

Your readers pay you for two things: emotional engagement and completion. You take them on a ride, bonded to a Lead, and then close the story arc.

Do those two things masterfully, and you'll have a hit. Keep doing it, and you'll have a career.

Helpful Hints for Plotters and Pantsers

It's entirely possible to plot a novel by starting with Transformation. You want to write about a certain character, say, a Kansas farm girl. You want to write a fantasy. You want to put this farm girl in all sorts of scary situations. Maybe even with a witch involved.

All that's roiling around in your head. You can stop right there and say to yourself, "What kind of feeling do I want readers to have at the end?"

You might answer, "I want them to feel like a great lesson has been learned."

What lesson?

Oh, that you shouldn't be so quick to want adventures. That maybe that could get you into trouble. Maybe home is the best place to be.

Hmm, there's no place like home.

Or, you might want to write about a survivor, like Richard Kimble. At the end, stronger. Imagine the circumstances of the Final Battle and Transformation. A fight with the bad guy? Where? In an occupied building?

Maybe so...

Super Structure Reminder

Readers love to worry. They love to worry about characters they are bonded with. What they worry about is how the Lead is going to ever get out of this story alive. Keep that question in their minds throughout, and give them a satisfactory conclusion at the end. They will thank you with their discretionary income.

A Final Word

Remember, Super Structure is all about making sure the power of story—the guts and blood and heart and emotion of it—connects to the reader in the most effective form.

You will never go wrong with the signposts.

But that does not mean you cannot try some other strategy if it seems right to you or if you simply want to mess around and see what happens.

Freedom of choice is your birthright.

However, my experience with the writers I've taught over nearly two decades is that a deep understanding of structure makes their stories better, clearer, stronger, more powerful.

Thus, the Super Structure Principle may be stated as follows: *The power of your story is directly proportional to the readers' experience of it, and the readers' experience is directly proportional to the soundness of the structure.*

When the structure feels "off," it dilutes the experience. Readers don't know why, they just feel it.

And when the structure is "on," readers don't notice it. They get pure story pumped into them without distraction or confusion.

Super Structure renders a solid story, every time.

Your job, then, is to fill it up with your own voice, vision, characters, dialogue, scenes, surprises, style.

When you pour *you* into structure, you create that unique product that makes for breakout authors and long-term careers.

Checklist of Reminders

Here for easy reference are the Super Structure Reminders that appear throughout this book:

DISTURBANCES DON'T HAVE to happen just at the beginning. You can sprinkle them throughout. When in doubt about what to write next, make more trouble.

WHEN YOU SHOW a character's humanity, you link her up to the collective unconscious of the audience. Don't be afraid to show humanity: caring, flaws, foibles, doubts, inner conflict, love, passion, anger, frailty as well as strength.

YOUR LEAD IS NOT JUST an action machine. She has beliefs and those beliefs get challenged by the story events.

THE "OFF SCENE" exercise is great at any point in your writing or planning. When you don't know what to write next, spend some time brainstorming what the other major characters are up to, unseen.

ANOTHER WAY TO describe a novel is that it is about a character who confronts challenges by *strength of will.* If the character takes no action, she's just being a wimp. Your Lead must never be a wimp! But sometimes things happen that are out of her control, and feel like a door is slamming behind her, as if in a haunted house. Think of these events as *plot thrust.*

REMEMBER: Trouble is your business! Don't be hesitant about plying your trade in every scene of your book.

THE BIGGEST CHANGES we make in our own lives occur when we are thrust into a crisis. Enduring fiction is built upon that same thing: it's about how a character, through force of will, fights life-threatening challenges and is transformed because of it. It's only when we feel we *must* change that we *do* change. The mirror moment makes that clear to the character and, most important of all, to the reader.

IF THE LEAD thinks only of himself the readers get a negative impression, subtle as that may be. Petting the dog adds a much-needed counter to that vibe. It can be as big as saving a life, or as small as giving a kind word to someone in need.

READERS DO NOT LIKE to see the Lead helped out of trouble via coincidence. So don't let this second doorway seem to offer that. A crisis or setback can happen that way, because it's not help. It's more trouble. But a discovery or clue ought to happen because the Lead has done something to find it, or earn it. It's the result of her efforts or cogitation that opens the door.

NO MATTER what kind of novel you write, the story ought to feel like the trash compactor in *Star Wars.* Your Lead is thrust into the situation of the novel. Then notices the walls starting to close in. In Act II, he's still got time to get out of danger. But in Act III time has run out. The walls are about to crush him.

SOME OF THE GREATEST ENDINGS--LIKE *Casablanca*—involve sacrifice. Rebirth can only follow death, and death is very often the sacrifice of the thing the Lead wants most. It may be his very life, as in *Spartacus* and *Braveheart*.

A NOVEL IS about a character using *strength of will* to fight the forces of death. This fight cannot just be analytical. We are moved to action through emotion, not simply logic.

ONE WAY TO describe the arc of a satisfying story is that it is, in the end, a quest for *courage*. In an outside-forces-type of ending, as in a thriller, the Lead must find the courage to fight against overwhelming odds. If he dies, we have one kind of tragedy, as in *Hamlet.* If it's inside, the Lead must find the moral courage to do the right thing. If he doesn't, the story becomes another kind of tragedy, the Lead left to suffer the consequences, as in *Hud,* the Paul Newman movie (based on *Horseman, Pass By* by Larry McMurtry).

READERS LOVE TO WORRY. They love to worry about characters they are bonded with. What they worry about is how the Lead is going to ever get out of this story alive. Keep that question in their minds throughout, and give them a satisfactory conclusion at the end. They will thank you with their discretionary income.

Author's Note

Thanks for reading my book. It's my great pleasure to help writers, so please take a moment to sign up for my occasional email updates. You'll be the first to know about my book releases and special deals. My emails are short and I won't stuff your mailbox, and you can certainly unsubscribe at any time.

You can sign up by going to the FREE BOOK page on my website:

JamesScottBell.com

Also, my comprehensive training course in the craft of bestselling fiction is now available. An investment that will pay off for your entire career.

https://knockoutfiction.teachable.com/p/novel

Thrillers by James Scott Bell

The Mike Romeo Thriller Series

Romeo's Rules
Romeo's Way
Romeo's Hammer
Romeo's Fight

"Mike Romeo is a terrific hero. He's smart, tough as nails, and fun to hang out with. James Scott Bell is at the top of his game here. There'll be no sleeping till after the story is over." - **John Gilstrap**, New York Times bestselling author of the Jonathan Grave thriller series

The Ty Buchanan Legal Thriller Series

Try Dying
Try Darkness
Try Fear

"Part Michael Connelly and part Raymond Chandler, Bell has an excellent ear for dialogue and makes contemporary L.A.

come alive. Deftly plotted, flawlessly executed, and compulsively readable. Bell takes his place among the top authors in the crowded suspense genre." - **Sheldon Siegel**, *New York Times* bestselling author

Stand Alone Thrillers

Your Son is Alive
Blind Justice
Don't Leave Me
Final Witness
Framed

Zombie Legal Thrillers

You read that right. A new genre. Part John Grisham, part Raymond Chandler—it's just that the lawyer is dead. Mallory Caine, Zombie at Law, defends the creatures no other lawyer will touch…and longs to reclaim her real life.

Pay Me In Flesh
The Year of Eating Dangerously
I Ate The Sheriff

About the Author

JAMES SCOTT BELL is a winner of the International Thriller Writers Award (*Romeo's Way*) and is the author of the #1 bestseller for writers, *Plot & Structure*. He studied writing with Raymond Carver at the University of California, Santa Barbara, and graduated with honors from the University of Southern California Law Center.

A former trial lawyer, Jim writes full time in his home town of Los Angeles.

For More Information
JamesScottBell.com

Made in the USA
San Bernardino, CA
25 March 2020